CONSOLATIONS
FOR MY SOUL

Thomas à Kempis
Author of *The Imitation of Christ*

CONSOLATIONS FOR MY SOUL

Meditations for the Earthly Pilgrimage
toward the Heavenly Jerusalem

being a translation of
SOLILOQUIUM ANIMAE

translated by
William Griffin

A Crossroad Carlisle Book
The Crossroad Publishing Company
New York

The Crossroad Publishing Company
16 Penn Plaza, 481 Eighth Avenue, New York, NY 10001

The text is typeset in 11/14 Adobe Caslon and 10/13 Bitstream Calligraphic 421. The chapter titles are in Post Antiqua.

Printed in the United States of America

Library of Congress Cataloging-in-Publication Data

Thomas, à Kempis, 1380-1471.
   [Soliloquium animae. English]
   Consolations for my soul : being a translation of Soliloquium animae /
Thomas à Kempis ; [edited and] translated by William Griffin.
     p. cm.
   Includes bibliographical references.
   ISBN 0-8245-2107-2
   1. Meditations.   I. Griffin, William, 1935- II. Title.
BV4830.T5513 2003
242 – dc22

2003023302

1 2 3 4 5 6 7 8 9 10   10 09 08 07 06 05 04

For Bernard Hassan

Contents

A Word from the Translator

"Consolation, not just a splash but a continuous flow — that, dear Reader, is what this little book is all about!" Thus the first words of *Consolations for My Soul*.

Kempis is gratefully remembered as author of *The Imitation of Christ*, a Vade Mecum, Baedeker, Michelin, Fodor, Zagat guide to the Soul on the tearful yet joyful trudge that is the Christian pilgrimage. Those who've been looking after their own souls or indeed the souls of others have relied on it for almost six centuries.

In the absence of further volumes of his in our bookstores, one would think that Kempis had just one book in him, but that wouldn't be the case. His *Omnia Opera* (*Complete Works*), when published a century ago, ran to seven volumes. Since then there hasn't been much translation, much commentary or criticism, complimentary or otherwise, of him or his works; with the exception of the *Imitation*, they've simply disappeared.

As for Kempis's other works, there are many. What euphonious titles! *Soliloquium Animae* (*Soliloquy of a Soul*), *Hortulus Rosarum* (*Garden of Roses*), *Vallis Liliorum* (*Valley of Lilies*). To mention only the most prominent. They're every bit as good as the *Imitation* and, beginning with this volume, they're making their way back into the English language.

This particular book is actually *Soliloquy*. But since it had to do not so much with soliloquy as with consolation, as Kempis proclaimed right from the start, the publisher suggested the title *Consolations*.

Yet there's something soliloquy about *Consolations*. Kempis is the only voice, but he's not an actor voicing his deepest thoughts to an expectant and appreciative audience. Rather he's more of a puppeteer, producing the voices of the Narrator (Kempis or Kempis-like character) speaking to the Soul (perhaps his own Soul), and the Soul speaking to the Lord.

One thing is certain. Everyone is opinionated, and everyone replies with a rush of vigor and a sense of certitude, occasionally accompanied by a thump or a thwack. That's to say, from the perspective of the twenty-first century and beyond, Kempis's technique is more Punch and Judy than Geppetto and Pinocchio, with a lot of sharp language, and not a little paddling.

Consolations was written for Kempis's own time, obviously, but, in this paraphrasal translation, it seems also to have been written for modern times. Sadly, the Soul and its travails haven't changed much over the centuries; just the metaphors and raggedy details.

Consolations has a unity all its own. It's a series of conferences — more accurately, notes for a series of conferences — for any of the variety of audiences he addressed regularly over the decades of his long life; he died in 1471 at the age of ninety-one. But these weren't aimed at beginners in the spiritual life; they were aimed at those who'd already had a good beginning; that's to say, those who'd more or less mastered the *Imitation*. *Consolations* is for those who've advanced — or fancied they've advanced — to a deeper appreciation and practice of the spiritual life.

Such consolations as the book offers were meant to help the Soul weather the storm and stress found in every healthy spiritual life. Indeed the word "consolation" as used by Kempis is just another word for Grace. As such, it's the lubricant for the Soul, the engine that has no parts. The more the Consolations or Graces, the fewer the squeaks and squawks, as the Soul wends its weary way to its own true home.

Information of historical and spiritual interest — perhaps more than the Reader wants to know — will occasionally be found throughout the book. If the translation proves interesting in general but troublesome here and there, the Reader may want to move right to a helpful essay: "Capital Sins and Capitalized Nouns," pages 60–63, "Translation, Literal or Paraphrasal," pages 107–109, "Gender, Historical or Contemporary," pages 118–121.

— WILLIAM GRIFFIN

August 8, 2003, the 932nd anniversary
of Kempis's death day in 1471,
which was also his birthday in the Lord

Thomas à Kempis

CONSOLATIONS FOR MY SOUL

Prologue

Consolation, not a splash but a continuous flow — that, dear Reader, is what this little book is all about. I've gathered together some helpful sayings and put them down with a few thoughts of my own. Why? Well, from time to time I've needed them at hand to soothe my troubled Soul. They're like an inviting meadow dotted with trees, a charming garden filled with flowers. Places both where, in times of necessity and uncertainty, I may come to read a book or admire a bloom. That's how I shed the storm and stress in my own life.

As for the sayings themselves, they're a mixed bunch, really; posies, nosegays. You'll hear my voice. I'm the one talking. I speak, I argue, I pray. Sometimes I talk to myself; sometimes, to an imaginary person; but always to God. The result is this slender volume, which I've turned out with a quiet but happy pen. It's helped me. Perhaps, dear Reader, it'll help you.

In this meadow and garden where practical wisdom grows, there are many, many lovely spots.

All that having been said, I hope no reader rises up in indignation against the hand that held the pen. It gave me such pleasure to put this collection together. But you may have to pardon my scattered style and ragged prose.

As for the stuff I chose to include, it's the simplest of advice, not the artful and artificial imitations of the amateur gardeners. But if you were to stumble upon some stinkweed, then snip it, pluck it, purge it from the earth! And if I were you, I'd have a word with the Gardener. No doubt He'll reply with an apology, saying that it'd strayed onto the property when He wasn't looking.

A final word, but to You, Dear God, Surgeon of All Trees, Pruner of All Plants. Up to this point in my human history so many judgments, no matter how probable they may have seemed at the time, turned out to be deceptive. That's why I keep running back to You as suppliant and disciple with one book after another, trying to undo my deceptions.

This one, *Consolations for My Soul*, I present to You today. If you consider it a worthy work, please accept it with my compliments. If so, then, for the benefit of the Faithful Reader, may You insinuate Yourself into each and every sentence, sentiment, serendipity. If not, just dump it in the basket, toss it in the trash.

A final prayer, but to You, Holy Father in Heaven. From Your vast celestial inventory grant me the favor of Your lingering presence in those rich passages of Scripture I mention along the way. They are, and will continue to be, my particular delights until mortality sets and eternity dawns.

In the meantime, in Your capacity as Landscaper, Designer, Gardener, do rake up, drag off, put the torch to, all the choke weeds that get in the way of a pleasant and productive spot. Meditating on the intimate and the divine — that's what I do there and indeed here in this book. To do that, my Soul has to be open, yet quiet, yet eager. But I can't be any of these without the sweet wildness of Your Consolations.

1

Taking the First Steps

Clinging to God — such a good thing!
(Psalm VUL 72:28; NRSV 73:28)

Letting go of the world, grabbing hold of You, Dear God —
what a daring thought! Who can ask for anything more? Certainly not the Psalmist, who composed many a sweet lyric in his
lifetime, but never a verse so brief, so sweet as the one above!
Soul so holy, Soul so timid, what are you waiting for? Sing out
with the Psalmist, "What a good thing it is, clinging to God!"
And just think what would happen if it ever came to pass?

You, GOD, You're mine — goodness, sweetness, all! When
Your name pops up, the conversation always takes a turn for
the better. Is it any wonder, then, why we Devouts talk about
You so much?

"WHERE'S MY HEART?" You ask in reply. It should be in the
world, on display, spread open for all to see. But no, as the
Psalmist sang, it's tucked away in Heaven, hidden from the
world (VUL 72:73; NRSV:25). And good thing it is too. Back
in the world, Falseness mummering as Goodness nailed You
to the cross a hundred times a day. But back in Heaven, my
own true home, everything is smooth and clear and cool.

"Soul so holy, Soul so devout, what's this I hear about you?" asked the Keeper of the Soul. "The stuff in the sky and the stuff on earth — they all appear so small to you? Well, why wouldn't they? They're so far away from God!

"You're searching for clues, aren't you?" asked the Keeper. "A name, an occupation, an address? It's God you're looking for, isn't it? What's that verse the Psalmist's so fond of? 'Lord, I love the furniture and finery of Your house, as well as the glorious lighting throughout!' (vul 25:8; nrsv 268).

"Well, just don't stand there!" shouted the Keeper. "Answer my questions! No, you don't actually have to answer them — a wink or a nod will do. Yes, I'll join you in your search. We'll look together. And what will we find in the end? Hopefully, your God and my God. And once we find Him, we'll put Him into protective custody and never let Him go!

"So, Soul so holy, Soul so suspicious, why are you scrounging around in my pockets? You think I have some clues I'm not going to share? Don't be silly! I know what you're thinking. You want to know why I say such nasty things to you. You want to see whether I'm really man enough to stand up to you. Well, I am. So what is it you want to grill me about? *Where's God? How to find God?*

"Perhaps, Soul so holy, Soul so hopeless, you should put the question to those who've heard Him and seen Him. Yes, they're the ones who know where He is.

"More to the point, ask Him yourself. He's the one who gives the really useful description, and He's the one, the only one, who fits the description. As to where He hangs his hat, ask Him. He'll give you directions; no doubt, very long and detailed ones; please do take notes.

"Who is He?

"'He's the one,' said the Psalmist, 'who teaches Humankind what there is to know in the world. Of course, He's also the one who puts the lash to Humankind for knowing too much about the world' (VUL 93:10; NRSV 94:10). That may be, said the Letter of James (4:6) and Peter's First (5:5), 'but He also gives His grace to the Humble.'

"Soul so holy, Soul so shy," said the Keeper, "the first steps are the hardest. There's His door. And there's the knocker on His door. Give it a rap. No, He doesn't have a majordomo — He answers the door Himself; that's to say, when He answers it at all. Give it another rap, and if He does open it, you'll discover all the holiness and all the hilarity of those who live there with Him. And you won't find that in my pockets, no matter how deep you dig!"

CLINGING, THE PRIMAL PRAYER POSITION

"Clinging" is a frequent and indeed continuing topic in Kempis's writings; especially in his collection of spiritual wisdom, *The Imitation of Christ.* "Clinging for dear life to a created thing is fatalistic. Clinging to Jesus is futuristic. Love Him and keep Him as your friend" (2:7).

"Those who want to walk with Me in the Garden have to leave behind at the gate all their worldly clingings — that's to say, all their diddly depravities and fickle affections, all their creature comforts and private stashes" (3:53).

In Old English the word "clinging" had unattractive meanings: *shrink, shrivel, wither.* In Middle English, literally it meant *glue, stick, adhere;* figuratively, it came to mean *adhere or be attached to in affection, fellowship, sympathy, practice, or idea.*

In Scripture "clinging" has a noble history. The Hebrew word *dvekut* means an intimate clinging to God, a favorite concept of the Psalmist's. One verse in particular stands out (VUL 72:28; NRSV 73:28), here variously translated in paraphrase. "Clinging to God — such a good thing!" "I like it here, clinging to the Lord — it's a nice, a comfortable place." "He clings to me and I to Him."

In the Gospel of Luke Jesus is recorded as saying that no one can serve two masters; "either he hates the one and loves the other, or he condemns the one and clings to the other" (16:13). According to Matthew (19:5) and Mark (10:7), when a man marries, he must uncling himself from his parents before he can cling himself to his wife.

At one point Kempis's prose turns to prayer. *Purify, glorify, clarify, vivify — with all Your powers — my spirit that it may cling to You with joyful hugs!* (3:34).

Back to this book. As far as Kempis is concerned, clinging is the archetypical spiritual act, the primal prayer position. And it's amazing how many ways he can describe "clinging" without actually using the word.

Parenthetically please note that references throughout to the *Imitation* come from my paraphrasal translation (San Francisco: HarperSanFrancisco, 2000). —W.G.

2

Hanging Around, Moping About

Don't be a slug!
The Prophets knew what they were talking about.

(Luke 24:25)

"So, Soul so holy, Soul so humble," said the Keeper, "now that you've discovered God in His lair, I know you'll want to tell the world. But perhaps, just perhaps, He'd prefer His privacy. Of course, there's the question about the sort of words one would use to describe God. And even if you could find the proper words, perhaps you should still keep them close to your vest. Yes, keep your door closed; the seal of faith, unbroken; the sanctuary veil, unparted; that sort of thing. But also, do consume the Holy Bread in the sacred precincts. Do enter the tabernacle. Do ascend to the upper room. Do enter the chamber of the King Eternal, the suite of the Bridegroom, a place where Love can truly reign."

"One can't always make a grand entrance," said the Keeper. "Remember that verse in Matthew? 'One doesn't just take bread baked for the tots and toss it to the dogs' (15:26).

"That's what the Lord said to *that Canaanite woman.* She was one of those impossible pagans with outrageous requests who dogged His footsteps while on earth. The Evangelist almost called her *that Canine woman.* But rereading that passage,

I find my wretched state now matches hers then. She replied humbly but firmly then; I can only hide behind her skirts.

"'Well that may be, Lord, but look at it from the pups' point of view. They have to scrap around for whatever the scraps. Then, with no warning whatsoever, from the Master's table above, come tumbling down as if in a rain, crumbs, morsels, tidbits of all sorts. Scrap no more! Scraps no more! It's manna from Heaven!'" (15:27).

"Well," said the Soul, "that saved her goose and now, dear Lord, that I'm hoving into Your merciful view, I hope it'll save mine. Yes, I'm hanging onto this verse from Matthew to save my eternal life.

"Like that feisty woman I have some impossibly small requests. From the banquet hall above, just one spark of Your mercy, that's all I need from Your roaring fire. From the wine cellar below, just one drop of Your house brand. From the shapely cruet, just one whiff of Your cologne! Fortified with these, O Lord, I now feel I may approach, safely, piously, Your lovable and frequent Consolation.

"So, SOUL SO FEARFUL and so fretful," asked the Keeper, "why are you hanging around, moping about, pretending you don't hear? There's Someone at the gate, Someone at the door. So, open it. Open it and greet Him as one long-lost friend to Another. As for me? Don't worry about me. I'll busy myself about.

"No, don't tell me you're tongue-tied, awestruck again. Just say the first thing that comes into your mind. Tell it as it is. But why would you? Who really can tell it as it is? And who can gather in one's arms the One who's greeting him so warmly?

"Well, if nothing's going to come out of your mouth but your bad breath, then you might as well puke, hurl, toss off whatever troubles you most deeply! It just might do you some good. And in a funny sort of way, it may just move you one step closer to Him."

"You can't possibly be in such a wretched state of Soul as you confess," said the Keeper, "and then deny it by quoting the Psalmist — or can you? 'Omniscience is a wonderful thing, but in Your case, Lord, it's more battlement than firmament. That's to say, looking down from Your impossible height, You see all my hiding places' (VUL 138:6–7; NRSV 139:6–7).

"Soul, so cowardly, Soul so cowering, if your resources aren't potent enough to slip through the flimsy defenses of your own spirit, whom the Creator and Vivifier of all spirits has created, how do you think to blow a hole in the wall of the Uncreated Spirit? I almost blush to say it! The Psalmist himself could barely whisper it 'O Lord, is there no one else like you? Who can compare with you? Who can stand up to you?'" (VUL 34:10; NRSV 35:10).

HOW TO READ A KEMPIS BOOK

How to read this book? Well, since this is a mystical treatise, one can begin anywhere — beginning, middle, or end. One thing is certain, the book isn't meant to be read from stem to stern in one sitting in hopeful expectation of intellectual enjoyment.

A little *lectio divina* would be more appropriate; that's to say, pause whenever you feel like it, and pray whatever you like. If you were to do that, Kempis, one of the great spiritual directors of all time, would be truly pleased!

3

Tracking God Down

Please, sir, if you've seen His body, tell me where it is.
(John 20:15)

"So, Soul so holy and so eloquent, as Keeper of your Soul, I've done all the talking. Now what do you have to say for yourself?"

"Well, Keeper of my Soul, I know you've been trying to be helpful but, I must say, you've been nothing but trouble. You've trashed my person. You've trashed my belongings. You've trashed my opinions. You've interrogated me to death about my one true self. But now, I have a question for you. Just who is this Uncreated Spirit?"

"To that, Soul so holy, I have but one reply. 'Don't complain to me. Complain to Him. He's the One you're looking for.'"

"Well, I know that."

"You're tracking God down, yes, but will running Him to ground be so easy?"

"Well, just don't drag out that shaggy sermon of yours, that old warhorse you use whenever you want to spread some consolation around."

"All right, I won't."

"But if you were going to preach to me, just what would that consolation be?"

"As Judith did say, 'Your Soul lives, O Lord' (12:4).

"As Jacob did say to that angelic galoot with whom he was wrestling in the dark, 'I'm not going to let you out of my grasp until you give me your blessing' (Genesis 32:26).

"As Mary Magdalen did say to the Gardener, who was really the Risen Lord, 'Please, sir, if you've seen His body, tell me where it is, and I'll see that it's properly buried' (John 20:15).

"That's what I'd say."

AGAIN, SOUL SO HOLY spoke up.

"As you can see, I'm in a froth of desire, laboring out of love for the Creator. What should I do?"

Again Keeper of the Soul spoke back.

"Something difficult, that's for sure, but I don't think you want to hear it."

"And what would that be?"

"I'd refer you to the Scriptures, where much of your investigation has taken place to date. Remember the Bride in the Canticles? 'Point him out to me,' she said, 'the one my Soul's in love with'" (VUL Canticle of Canticles 1:6; NRSV Song of Solomon 1:7).

"Yes," replied Soul so holy, "I think I already know the Person I'm looking for and what good He'll do for me and why I shouldn't broadcast it to the world."

"Perhaps that's the best thing to do," replied Keeper of the Soul. "Remember the Lord in Isaiah? 'Heart, keep your secret; no need to spread the word abroad' (24:16).

"Well, all that should be encouraging, but I'm afraid it's made me discouraged. The bigness of Him, the smallness of me, why should He care about a flyspeck like myself?

I'm giving up the search. I no longer have the strength, the appetite, for it."

"Yes, it's such a trudge," replied Keeper of the Soul. "It was for the Psalmist too. 'I enter in the sanctuary, the holy place of God' (VUL 72:17; NRSV 73:17). Do as he did, and you'll come to understand. And don't worry, my friend. Sad as you are, and sad as I am at your sadness, I won't spill the beans."

KEMPIS AND THE BIBLE

Thomas à Kempis (1379/80–1471) is acknowledged as a spiritual master today, but for centuries his reputation was tarnished by the charge that in his works he quoted the Bible few times and, hence, couldn't have known all that much about the Book of Books, which contained all that needed to be known.

Actually, just the opposite is true. He was a copyist by profession. During his long and full life he made four handwritten copies of the complete Bible, including what's referred to today as the Apocrypha.

When his *Opera Omnia* (*Complete Works*) were published in seven volumes (1902–1922), the back matter of each volume included a list of Scripture verses quoted or alluded to. In the *Imitation,* for example, Kempis made a thousand such references. Most were allusions; that's to say, a play on the words of each reference as it suited the particular Kempis context.

(In addition to the scriptural authors, Kempis also quoted, often not citing the source, such classical Greek and Latin authors as Aristotle, Seneca, Ovid, Virgil, Cicero, Lucan, and Dionysius.)

What Bible did Kempis use?

In the fourth century Pope Damasus (AD 366–384) asked his talented secretary, Jerome, if he wouldn't take on the humongous task of standardizing the Latin Bible texts and rendering the whole into Latin for a lowbrow audience (Vulgate); that would match the lowbrow Greek Bible (Koine). And so he did.

Not only did Kempis copy the Bible professionally and use it editorially in his books, he also used it devotionally for a lifetime as an Augustinian monk.. Hence, his knowledge of the Bible may be said to be intimate, biblical quotations and allusions running through his works like golden threads. For example, in *Consolations for My Soul,* which is half the length of the *Imitation,* he made three hundred quotations or allusions.

Please note that in a few recent versions of the *Imitation,* translators have footnoted or endnoted quotations and allusions, and left it at that. In my translations of Kempis, however, rather than doing that, I've inserted each and every allusion into the Kempis text. And in trying to reproduce the flavor of the Latin original, I didn't just resort to plugging in snippets from an approved English translation of the Vulgate (alas, there isn't one at the moment); rather I've translated the original Latin Vulgate texts into my own paraphrasal English and slipped them into the English translation of Kempis without so much as leaving a seam behind. For better or worse.

The Reader will surely have noticed by now that Scripture sources have been included in the text in parentheses, and they are presented in three different ways.

First, when Bible book, chapter, and verse are the same in both the Latin Vulgate and the New Revised Standard Version, the Bible versions aren't named.

Second, when the Bible books are the same, but the chapter and verse have different numbers, then both VUL and NRSV are given; for example, (Psalm VUL 7:28; NRSV 7:29).

Third, when the Bible book is the same but has a different name, then both are given; for example, (VUL Book of Wisdom 12:15; NRSV Wisdom of Solomon 12:15).

Please note that references to the New Revised Standard Bible merely indicate where the same sentiment, but not necessarily the same wording, may be found.

—W.G.

4

Being Tracked Down by God

The Lord's coming. Don't worry. You look fine.
(1 John 2:28)

After the passage of some time, Keeper of the Soul spoke again.

"This is our secret place, yours and mine. For friends only! That's what our conversation will be. A little giddiness from you, a little arrogance from me, what does that amount to between friends? Let's just enjoy this warm chatsworthy place."

"But what if He comes?"

"If He does pop in, make another of His surprise visits, I think we can squeeze in a bit to make some room for Him?"

"We can put Him right between us."

"Remember, if He has something to say," said Keeper, "give Him the floor."

"I think I could bite my tongue until He's finished."

"Sometimes it's just polite conversation," said Keeper. "Other times, though, He's just too heady for my taste!"

"What do you mean by that?"

"It just doesn't matter what we say," said Keeper; "His virtues and His magnificence sail on undiminished."

"Are the Scriptures any help here?"

"Sometimes," said Keeper, who proceeded to give some instances.

"'If the Heaven of heavens couldn't catch the drift,' as Solomon put it on a different occasion, then my poor descriptions won't do the trick (VUL 2 Paralipomenon 6:18; NRSV 2 Chronicles 6:18).

"'I've heard it all already,' the dear Habacuc cried out, 'and I'm about to toss my victuals.' 'My teeth chatter when I hear their voices'" (3:6).

"Well," asked Soul so holy, "when our turn to talk comes, what'll we say?"

"Ask Him a question."

"I have so much to ask!"

"Ask the first one that comes into your head," replied the Keeper sensibly.

"So what's Your name?"

"'I AM WHO AM' — that's what the Lord said to the Exodist — 'and I don't have a twin'! (3:14)

"'Always the first and always the last, always the oldest and always the youngest — that's who I am, creating everything and governing its operation.'

"As John wrote in the Apocalypse (1:17), 'I live,' said the Lord, 'I shall reign until the last day, and even beyond, if all were known' (22:5).

"As Solomon put it in the Canticle of Canticles, 'Behold, your Beloved Bridegroom is speaking with you'" (2:10).

"I'm not one of your wandering minstrels or maundering wastrels," replied the Lord, who was masquerading as the Keeper of the Soul. "I'm unique among uniques. I don't need friends or companions. I'm thoroughly at home conversing with Myself. Solo. Soliloquy. No symphony for me."

"But if You were to ask," replied the Soul, who hadn't a clue as to who was talking with him, "I could be good friends with you. As the Psalmist has said, 'I like it here, clinging to the Lord, it's a nice place, a comfortable place'" (VUL 7:28; NRSV 7:29).

"I come and I go when I want," replied the Lord. "And yes, since you're about to ask, such is My Omnipresence that I do occasionally meet Myself coming and going."

"Not so fast," replied the Lord, alluding to the Dear Isaiah. "Hold your horses!" (28:10). Yes, He pops in and, yes, He pops out. So, Soul so joyous, Soul so jumpy, it drives you crazy, and so it drives Me crazy too. One moment He brings you to the heights; the next, He sends you to the depths. But love, and the expectation of love, gently fill the intervals in.

"NICE THING about His being gone, dear Keeper, is that when He returns, He brings the most wonderful gifts. Pretty flowers. Precious stones. But it's not so much the gifts that are so special; it's the sentiments that come with them. Nothing in creaturedom tops His love. Indeed the rest of creaturedom looks rather measly in comparison.

"Yes, He's touched me, there's no doubt about that. It's a touchy, tactile sort of feeling. A deep embrace, yes, but one that doesn't rumple, dishevel, the Soul. This, in sharp contrast with the way creatures touch each other. Every time I catch myself in damp embrace with one of them, I end up needing a bath."

"WHAT'S THERE IN HEAVEN FOR ME?" asked the Psalmist. "For that matter, what's left on Earth for me?" (VUL 72:25–

26; NRSV 73:25–26). God of my heart, and my part, God in eternity!

"IF YOU'RE GOING to get involved with the Beloved," said the Keeper, "there's something you should know. He's bigger and better than the rest of us, and we don't know how He does it. Yes, He's unflappable, unfluffable, indeciperable, indescribable — or is He? Well, I don't know. Perhaps it's just that our poor language doesn't have enough bounce to do Him justice.

"Nonetheless, all that having been said, He remains quite a likable and approachable fellow, who likes to hang out from time to time and chew the rag about things spiritual. Yes, He can't be understood in the conventional sense but, in a wonderful sort of way, He can be loved. He's captivated by the love of friendship, and He continually proves Himself a true friend. And He wants you to prove the same.

"Knowing you yearn for Him makes Him feel all the more sought after. Knowing your prayerful affections for Him, He thumps on your door all the more loudly. Knowing you're waiting for Him, He hastens back all the more quickly.

"And that's all I know about Him.

"So," asked the Keeper, "has anything I've been saying made sense to you at all?"

"Maybe, maybe not," said the Soul. "But I do want to leave you with this prayer."

May the Mysterious One Who deliberately fails to cover His tracks lead you on a merry chase!

And now that teacherly types like myself have failed utterly and miserably to help you in your quest, may He Himself take you in hand and lead you to His Heavenly Home!

5

Running from God

*Falling into the hands of an angry God
is not a happy experience!*
(Hebrews 10:31)

Dear God, there's so much about You to love, but such a lot to fear. Such a predicament! The person who knows how to love You rejoices, but the person who doesn't know what love is runs for his life! Fear without love? But who can live like that? A blockhead? A lunatic?

DEAR READER, falling into the hands of an angry God is, as the Letter to the Hebrews puts it, ghostly, ghastly, god-awful! (10:31).

As the Psalmist asked it, quaking in his boots as he sang it, who can imagine the size of Your wrath? (VUL 89:11–12; NRSV 90:11–12).

Who can withstand the blast when You come in judgment? (3:2).

AT THE FINAL SPECTACLE, Reader dearest, the lion will roar, but you — the best you'll be able to do is croak! For this lovely image we have the dear Isaiah to thank (5:29). The fire will dance, God's sword will flash; the Psalmist again (7:13).

At the shout of His voice, all the inhabitants of the earth will cover their ears. All the fundaments of the earth will crack. At this horrific prospect who isn't fouling his garments?

DEAR GOD, how will anyone escape Your clutches? If a person were to find refuge under a mighty slab, You'd thunder over it, and his fortitude would crumble. If a person were to hide in a cavern or high on a mountain, wherever it is, he'll meet his Maker for better or worse. And he'll continue to be the object of Divine Wrath until he looks into what it'll take to arrive at Final Peace.

ONE THING'S CERTAIN, Lord. There's no place where a person can find refuge from Your face. Everything's open to Your eyes — there's nothing without drape or covering, so the Letter to the Hebrews has promised. So much for human exteriors. But what about the interiors? Alas, Your eyes penetrate these as well (4, 13). The most subtle of thoughts You see through. As for the Secrets of the Universe, well, they're still secrets to us, but to You, Lord, they're only scrims through which You peek as much as You like.

DEAR LORD, how terrifying it is to be a sinner! The hard-hearted and the hard-headed will be especially hard hit! Those who are evil and proud of it will be devastated. These last the Psalmist had no use for (VUL 51:3; NRSV 52:3), nor did the kindly old Proverbialist think they had much of a chance (2:14). Their excuses? *God has no eyes* and *God has no brain.* Pathetic! Even if He didn't, He wouldn't have missed much. Evil persons aren't that much to look at, nor are they what one might call intellectuals! What would He see? What would He know?

Dear Lord, it's Your own fault, You know. You've taken Your time in making the Return Trip. Meanwhile, the Evil Ones fill their time juggling silly syllogisms, giving not a thought to the End Game that's sure to come (Psalm 10:11).

You will be coming, won't You, Dear Lord — but as You said through the Evangelist Luke (12:40), at an hour we'll never guess? Well, that's when we'll get caught in the traps of our very own making. And like felons everywhere, once we've been snared, we'll proclaim our innocence, wondering what we did that was so wrong.

Now we laugh at You, Dear Lord, but soon You'll return the compliment.

Now we malign You, but soon You'll malign us.

Now we hold Your justice in contempt; soon You'll hold our foolishness in contempt; that, the Proverbialist has surely promised (1:24).

Now when You speak, we feel our deafness coming on; but soon we'll cry out in the forest, and You'll have trouble finding Your ear trumpet.

Now we turn Your story into make-believe. But soon You'll turn our behavior into make-good.

So, my fine fiery Friend, Your sermon breathes destruction, and Your words'll scorch the Impious and brand the Incredulous. What will the Brain-Proud or Brain-Drained among us have to say then, or the Muscle-Bound or Weak-as-Water? And then, of course, us. How will we all respond when we hear the Final Trump, when that Lord God of ours appears in majesty with Angels on one side, Archangels on the other?

THE DIFFERENCE A WORD MAKES

The word *sermo* is Latin for, well, "sermon." It appears at the beginning of the last paragraph of the previous selection, "Running from God." "Your sermon breathes destruction...." But *sermo* could have been translated into English any number of other ways.

According to *Lewis and Short's Latin Dictionary* (1889), which covers ancient Latin, including the classical period, *sermo* had at least the following meanings. A continued speech, talk, conversation, discourse. A set conversation, learned talk, discourse, disputation, discussion. An utterance, declaration, speech, remark. Ordinary speech, talk, conversations, language. Prose. Conversational verse, satire. Common talk, report, rumor. A manner of speaking, mode of expression, language, style, diction. A language, speech.

According to *A Glossary of Later Latin: To 600 A.D.*, compiled by Alexander Souter (1949), *sermo* came to mean the Latin *Verbum* and the Greek *Logos;* that's to say, the Word of God in Scripture, Tertullian, and Cyprian.

According to *Mediae Latinitatis Lexicon Minor (A Short Dictionary of Medieval Latin)*, compiled by J. F. Niermeyer (1999), the word came to mean sermon or homily.

Well, one way or another, *sermo*, in each and every instance means some or all of the above. But a translator has to whittle the meaning down to one English word. One that could be understood by the many and varied audiences Kempis addressed over his long and full life. The Augustinian monastery. The Brothers and Sisters of the Common Life. Whoever happened to show up in Zwolle on any given day, seeking the practical wisdom he was rumored to be dishing out to the spiritually hungry. And at the same time an English word that can be understood today, some six hundred years later.

Consolations is something of a wisdom book in that it contains the sort of biblical wisdom found in Proverbs, Ecclesiastes, Jesus Son of Sirach, the Letter of James. Yes, this book contains wisdom in lots of short takes, grouped under a number of pertinent headings. The sayings were the product of the common thoughts and writings of Geert Grote (died 1384), Gerard Zerbolt of Sutphen (died 1398), Florent Radewijns (died 1400), Kempis (died 1471), and Lord knows how many others. As head of the copy room, librarian, archivist, Kempis had access to all of this golden material, and to it he no doubt added his own particular favorites.

Back to chapter 5. *Sermo* as translated paraphrasally, with the Soul apparently edgy about something the Lord had said in a previous chapter, can be rendered something like the following.

"Your sermon breathes destruction...."

"Your sermonizing blisters our horny hide...."

"You've sermonized us to a crisp once again...."

"You've toasted us up quite nicely this time...."

—W.G.

6

Hurrying toward Doom

First off, round up the usual suspects.

(Matthew 13:30)

Yes, Dear Lord, there are indeed some things we dunderheads know for certain.

All those who wreaked havoc with Your words will drop their chops.

All those who tore Your devouts into shreds will themselves be shredded into confetti.

All those who stuffed their conscience with logical and lyrical swill and soaked themselves in vanities and lecheries will be overcome with confusion.

All those who relaxed the reins of flesh will feel their limbs bound with tightest cord.

All those who played around with musical instruments like Job will howl pathetically at the moon (21:12–13).

When Joy breaks the rules, then Grief is the one who rules.

All of our drinking companions will soon be tied up into bundles, ready to hiss and crackle in the Final Fire; that's to say, if Matthew's parables about Hell have any truth in them (13:30).

All those whom Love entangled in faulty embrace, the avenging flame will barbecue in punishment.

How wretched and wrong-headed can people get? asked Paul in Galatians, and he was as good a name-caller as ever has been (3:1, 3).

Crazy as loons, blind as bats! Lovers of the world we live in, what are you doing and what are you pretending to do? How will you react to the wrath of the Lord?

Why are you harrying and hurrying toward your Final Doom? Each moment's worth of worldly pleasure is a tiptoe toward eternal torment.

At each pinprick of penance you cry ouch, but what'll you yowl at the eternal flame of Gehenna?

You've spent a lifetime enlivening your mind, but you haven't spent a moment prolonging the life of your soul!

So what does all this amount to?

Unless you turn yourself around and do the penance the Psalmist harped on (7:13), you're toast, toast burnt to a crisp!

JUST THINKING of my last day, my last hour, I turn to jelly! It's too late to pray. It's time to be judged. Everyone gets the justice he or she deserves.

O God so holy and God so strong, don't despair of me! Don't hand me over to a bitter death! Instead, give me a decent place of penance where I can weep quietly over my sins. The last thing I want is to be dismissed from the Light.

PURGATORY, REAL OR IMAGINED

For Kempis in the fifteenth century, Purgatory was just as vivid a reality as Heaven and Hell, and hence an integral part of his spirituality.

As a place Purgatory was halfway between Earth and Heaven. As a time, it was halfway between Earthly Death and Eternal Life. As a reward, it wasn't quite Heaven and not quite Hell. As an answer, it came after the question, *If the Soul at the moment of death didn't go to Heaven or Hell, then where did it go?* It's chief industry: prison management or, perhaps more nicely put, refinery maintenance. Its population: unknown, but presumed large, and definitely transitory.

In the Christian Scriptures there are two references that point directionally toward Purgatory.

In the Old Testament, specifically in 2 Maccabees (12:39–45), Judas Maccabeus offered prayers and sacrifices for the souls of some heroic soldiers, even though they'd died with pagan symbols in their pockets. Such an infraction should've sent them to Gehenna, but the good Judas, no doubt under the inspiration of the Spirit, thought that their act wasn't evil enough to send them to that hellish place.

In the Gospel of Matthew (12:32), Jesus referred to sins that would be forgiven in the here-and-now and in the hereafter, and to other sins that wouldn't be forgiven either in time or eternity.

The inevitable conclusion? Purgatory is the product of, if not Scripture, then Tradition.

What gave legs to Purgatory were the sermons and writings of the Fathers of the Church right from the beginning. Tertullian, Origen, Cyprian, Ephram, Ambrose, Augustine, Chrysostom.

What gave strength to Purgatory were the syllogisms of the medieval philosophers (Thomas Aquinas, chief among them) that set the stage for two ecumenical councils of the church. Lyons (1245 and 1274) included a description of Purgatory among its many sections; Florence (1438–1445), in Kempis's own lifetime, firmed up what is now the Catholic and Orthodox understanding of Purgatory; that's to say, it's a doctrine, not a dogma.

But what truly gave wings to Purgatory were the artists. Canvases and tapestries galore, portraying the Final Judgment, with the Saints bubbling at the top and the Devils gargling at the bottom, but in the capacious middle were the Sinners undergoing some sort of ugly purgative processing.

In fourteenth-century Italy Dante Alighieri composed *La Divina Commedia,* an epic poem in three parts, the second of which is *Purgatorio.* Together with *Inferno* and *Paradiso* they form a triumphant work of the human imagination!

In fifteenth-century Europe mystery plays — short plays about episodes in the Scriptures, often robust, often rollicking — went spilling from church sanctuaries out into courtyards. Among the favorite topics, Purgatory.

In Chester, England, just such a play appeared in a cycle of twenty-five; written sometime between 1325 and 1375, they were produced over a three-day period by various guilds in that prosperous city. The Cooks and Innkeepers made "The Harrowing of Hell" their signature work.

Among the characters in the play, which was set in Hell, were Adam, Isaiah, Simeon the Just, John the Baptist, Seth, David, Enoch, and Elias. Vying for these souls were Satan ("Prince of Pain," as Jesus called him) and Jesus Himself (a "Fairly Fearsome Freak," as Satan called him). High point of the play had to be Jesus' grand, sweeping entrance as "King of Bliss," shouting "Open Hell gates anon!"

Alas, not all the souls were harrowed, rescued, saved. At least one woman didn't make the cut. She was a loud-mouthed alewife who must have reminded the men in the audience of their wives. She took over the stage, lamenting her parlous state at great length. Finally, to shut her up, Satan personally welcomed her, and one of his minions approached her as though she were the trophy bride of his malodorous dreams.

Yes, Purgatory was an integral part of Kempis's spirituality, and he mentioned it in this and his other works any number of times, but often not by the name Purgatory. He preferred to describe the purgatorial experience. For example, "a quiet, decent, penitential sort of place where I can weep quietly over my sins" (*Consolations*, 2).

—W.G.

7

Praying through
the Loneliness

Don't turn Your back on me, Lord!
(Psalm VUL 12:1; NRSV 13:1)

Dear God of mine, I've stained my life with many sins, but don't forget to count the tears I've shed for them.

Goodness is no longer domiciled with me; she decided to take a hike. But what can I expect? As long as I have to drag around in these baggy human clothes, at least according to the Apostle Paul to the Romans, I'm never going to be free of sins at all (7:18).

And so it is, dear Lord, not a day passes that I don't do bad. The graver the sin, the likelier it is that I've let it pass without the appropriate confessing and contriting.

How can this be?

Well, when I get going, get totally involved in the seriosities and curiosities of life in this world, I just can't be expected to stop on a pinhead and shed a salutary tear, can I?

But isn't that always the way? Sins mount up in the dark, multiply vigorously, clogging the Fountains of Grace, fouling the streams of Divine Consolation.

A question arises.

Is this behavior of mine really an evil thing and, if so, isn't it just a minor infraction, a peccadillo, a venial sin?

Well, I've asked the question as if I didn't know the answer already, but I do. Yes, this is a great evil, dear God of mine. But how great is it? It's so great that it very quickly passes from my heart's remembrance without my having to feel the slightest tingle of remorse.

"DEAR LORD," I cry out with the Psalmist, "You haven't turned your back on me, have You?" (VUL 12:1; NRSV 13:1).

Yes, I admit to playing hide-and-seek with You and, yes, I'm still sinning my way merrily through life.

But You know, Lord, You used to be such a chatterbox! I couldn't turn You off, but now You don't say a thing to me, don't even acknowledge my existence.

"Where's Your rod, Your switch, Your scourge?" Again, I cry out the Psalmist's cry (VUL 22:4; NRSV 23:4). I wait, I cringe, I shudder, but the crack of the whip never comes.

You used to stream past my eyes, images and images of Judgment and Hell, but now nothing. Why is that? If these horrific scenes were still vivid before me, do You think I'd have been so negligent, so haphazard, about my behavior?

I mean, isn't there in Your treasury a Grace of Doing Better? And if there is, shouldn't You be telling me more about it? I suppose now You're going to tell me that You're just being patient with me. Well, that's like paying me out enough rope to hang myself. But is that what You want? If You really want to be a help, just jump on me and rattle my bones the next time You catch me in major neglect!

But You know what I really think? I think that if You don't sting the living daylights out of me, then I'll hold You personally responsible for my moral corruption, such as it was, is, and ever shall be!

YES, LORD, I know that no sin of mine, however large or small, will pass unnoticed, unavenged, unsatisfied. But wouldn't it be better if there were tears, big fat mournful tears streaming from my eyes? And wouldn't it be far better if these tears were spontaneous, not beaten out of me?

On my part the effort would be brief and, on Your part, from the judgment point of view, I mean, wouldn't the satisfaction be — ahem — just as satisfactory? And reconciliation between You and me be just as easy?

SINS, VENIAL AND MORTAL

Sin runs through Kempis's writings as it runs through all life, seeking whom it may devour. The battle against it is never-ending, never seems noble, always results in a bloody nose. Yes, as Kempis saw it, dealing with sin occupied much of an individual's spiritual life.

But, as the readers of *Consolations* may realize by now, Kempis has said, in a variety of different ways, that Jesus is quicker to forgive than the sinner to confess. This isn't to say that Kempis didn't know what the Bible had to say about sin.

In the Old Testament sin appeared as an act of disobedience (Genesis 2:16–17; 3:11; Isaiah 1:2–4; Jeremiah 2:32); as an insult to God (Numbers 27:14); as something detested and punished by God (Genesis 3:14–19; 4:9–16);

---

as injurious to the sinner (Tobit 12:10); as something to be expiated by penance (Psalm 1:19).

In the New Testament Paul portrayed sin as a transgression of the law (Romans 2:23; 5:12–20); a servitude from which we're liberated by Grace (Romans 6:16–18); a disobedience (Hebrew 2:2) punished by God (Hebrews 10:26–31).

John described it as an offense against God; a disorder of the will (John 12:43); an iniquity (1 John 3:4–10).

Jesus came, He said, to promulgate a new law more perfect than the old; that's to say, stressing the importance of internal acts to a degree hitherto unknown. In the Sermon on the Mount, He condemned as sinful many acts that'd been judged honest and righteous by the doctors and teachers of the Old Law. In particular, He singled out for particular denunciation hypocrisy, scandal, infidelity, and the sin against the Holy Spirit. In net He taught that sins came from the heart (Matthew 15:19–20).

Early on in the Christian era, theologians began to distinguish between serious and not-so serious sins; that's to say, between major and minor, or mortal and venial, sins.

In the fourth century Augustine defined *mortal sin* as "something said, or something done, or something desired — a thought, word, or deed — that was contrary to the eternal law." It's a voluntary act. It's a choice of, instead of a heavenly God, an earthly good, real or imagined. It's a major crack-up, not a fender-bender. It's a major obstacle, not a minor detour. It's a major insult, not a minor misunderstanding. Whatever else it is, it's an aversion, a turning away, from God, our soul's true home.

Venial sin is an aversion from God too, but only a momentary detour from the straight and narrow. It sends us off on a toot, but doesn't prevent us from arriving more or less surely at our Final Destination. It may put a dent or two into Charity but doesn't crumple the buckler altogether. It may drain off some precious Grace from the heavenly font, but doesn't deprive the soul of the Grace it needs to live. Best of all, it's reparable, mendable, fixable. That's what *venial* means, and that's why it merits temporal, not eternal, punishment.

Needless to say, both mortal and venial sins can be forgiven, and Kempis seemed to make this message clear on his every page. Indeed in all of his writings he spent much of his time as something of a border collie, nipping at the heels of sinners, trying to coax them back to the fold, and back to the Good Shepherd who awaited them with open arms. It's what spiritual masters have been doing for centuries. —W.G.

8

Praying through the Pain

Pain is my constant companion.
(Psalm VUL 37:18; NRSV 38:17)

Don't spare the rod, Lord! Make my eyes sting, my skin flare up, my tongue crack! What do I care?

As FOR MY FAULTS, sins, negligences in the past, Lord, do You really need to store them up, keep them on my account? If You continue to hoard them, then what else can I think but that You plan to use them against me, to hand me over to the torturers to extract my debt, right down to the last bloody drop. Just as You handed Your Son over to the soldiers to exact the redemption; that's the way Matthew told it in his Gospel (5:26).

Isn't it better to pay off less than is owed now but in a more salubrious way than I've paid off before? What I mean to say is, aren't purgative tears now better than purgatorial torments later?

Now's THE TIME for me to wail my head off as though I were chief — and indeed sole — mourner at my own funeral. A siren as long as my list of sins! Many are the sins I have to mourn, but to smile I have no reason whatsoever.

DARKNESS OF HEART and wetness of conscience — instances of vice, yes, but also occasions of grace — they persuade me to moan and to groan, flooding my eyes with tears. Odd thing, though, they often propel me out of a jam, out of a bind.

ALWAYS COOKING UP TEMPTATIONS? It'd be funny if it weren't so pathetic!

"SPARE ME, O LORD," as Job, another of Your holy screamers, cried out; "spare me!" (7:16).

Yes, Lord, I'll cry if that's what You want me to do. I can turn it on, and I can turn it off. No great thing. But why? Because it's time to cry! Time to open the floodgates!

SOME RANDOM THOUGHTS.

Happy the hour when sorrow for sins came into my life!

Blessed are the tears that erupt from contrition, scouring every stain from my soul.

SUPPOSE SOMEONE WANTED to discuss the abysmal state of my Soul, could that person do it fully and fairly without delving into my dirty laundry?

My God, True God, True Light, illumine all the dark corners of my heart. Incinerate all the stains of my mortality in a blast of ardor and judgment.

It's Yours to give a new heart, to create a clean heart, to prepare an out-of-the-way place. A place for You to get some rest. A tabernacle to suit Your station. Godliness becomes You, and cleanliness becomes my conscience.

YOU DON'T ENTER a house that's been neglected, dear Lord, or so my sources tell me, and You often leave an establishment where animals've had the run of the halls. But I worry that

You think my home is something like either of these. Well, nothing could be further from the truth. My home, my cell — that's to say, my room within a room, my heart, my soul — is a fairly clean and rather clement place where I repair to make up for my ruinous behavior.

SOME FURTHER THOUGHTS.

Unhappy the person who gets in the way of Your runaway ire, for You'll make short work of him!

Peace to the person upon whom You condescend to call and with whom You'd be glad to spend some quality time.

AS FOR ME, I'm just a wretch, a frightened prey in a field of traps, an exhausted prisoner with the hounds on his trail.

What kind of advice do You have for a person like me? What remedy is there for me unless I raise my bloodshot eyes to You! Unless I make such a fuss as to be heard in Highest Heaven! All of which means only one thing — to sacrifice one's self relentlessly to prayer.

When temptation swoops down, something has to be done. Prayer has to be siphoned to You! I have to prostrate myself before the Divine Tribunal. But if I got involved in these penitential activities, wouldn't I be drowning myself in prayer?

Where can I expect to find such a gush of Humility and Tears? Only at Your house, Lord, where Mercy and Redemption are always in plentiful supply. That's where the Psalmist has pointed me, and he if anybody should know (VUL 129:7; NRSV 130:7).

Lord God, Giver of all grace, grant me to cry with dignity and to cry for as short a time as possible. Yes, castigate me for all my sins, those that lurk in the shadows as well as those that prance about in the sun, and, yes, I'll bite my tongue while You do it.

In conclusion, Lord, we've talked all these things to death, haven't we? All I have to do now is do them. And why wouldn't I? They'll restore to me Lost Grace and prepare me for Found Grace.

ROOM WITHIN A ROOM

At an international congress of itinerant evangelists meeting in Amsterdam in 1986, an ecumenical council really, many came from the nonindustrialized, underdeveloped countries of Africa and Asia. Of these some were astounded by a curious phenomenon taking place in the hotel lobbies. A large door opened revealing a room, a number of evangelists entered the room, the door shut behind them. Next time the door opened, the evangelists were nowhere to be seen. "Where did they go?" Upstairs, actually. The room, the disappearing room, was an elevator.

Kempis had a "magic" room too. Often after dinner in his Augustinian monastery, the monks met in the recreation room for some pleasant conversation. He joined in for a few minutes and then excused himself, saying he had an appointment to keep, something about meeting a friend.

Kempis returned to his room (his monastic cell, actually) and shut the door. Then he fell on his knees and entered the room within his room — that's to say, his Soul — praying until his friend arrived; Jesus Himself. Perhaps this passage from the *Imitation* will help.

"The outside world? You know where that's at already. But as to the whereabouts of the inside world, do you have a clue? No matter. The Kingdom of God'll find you. How? The 'Peace and Joy in the Holy Spirit,' as Paul wrote to the Romans (14:17), comes only to the Pious; that's to say, only to those who invite Him.

"Clear out the rubbish within, then, and prepare a cool bare place. Christ'll come and take up residence. He'll furnish it with 'all of his glory,' as the Psalmist has sung (44, 14), and make it a warm chatsworthy spot. Visit Him whenever you like. Feel at home there. It's your own true home at last. Who would've believed?" (2:1).

"Whenever you pray," Matthew recorded the Lord as saying on the Mount, "go to your room and shut the door behind you. Then pray to the Father, and He'll respond, and no one else'll be the wiser" (6:6).

The same sentiments run through *Consolations*. The Soul and the Lord — friends forever. They don't meet as much as either would like, and both are verbal about it. An odd couple. Indeed they remind one of *The Odd Couple*. —W.G.

9

Sinking beneath the Waves

You have the advantage of me, Lord,
dropping in on my imperfections like this.
(Psalm VUL 138:16, NRSV 139:16)

Ah, Lord God, the questions that plague me!
What will become of me if I die today?
When will I finish the repair of my life?
Why do things never become better?
How can I get the upper hand on everything I touch?

EVEN AS I ASK these questions, the sort of questions the
Psalmist always asked, "I feel I'm sinking beneath the waves"
(VUL 68:3; NRSV 69:2). You'd think that by this time in my
life I'd have climbed out of the hole, made some progress,
reached some new plateau. But I just don't have a hope in the
world. I mean, all I want to do is become a friend of Yours.
Instead, desperation upon desperation is dumped upon me,
and rightly so. It all began with an itch. I scratched, but the
itch has inched its way around my Soul until now it's fully
inflamed.

OF COURSE, I could begin again. I could say, Now's the time.
"Any time," wrote Paul in his Second to the Corinthians, "is

a good time to make a change" (6:2). But just as soon as I say this, Sin knocks on the door. Enter the Enemy, the Evil One. I suppose I could object, but my generally tolerant attitude toward Evil grabs me in a most ungentle way, pins my arms, presses me painfully, until all I can do is scream, scream for help!

You see how it is with me, Lord. Every which way I turn, I encounter rejection, rejection and dejection. Raise your right hand, Lord, I beg you. Free me from all the things that've cut me off from You. I'm afraid to do it by myself because they're so drop-dead intimidating.

What little Good Counsel I used to have has fled from me. And such Fortitude as I used to count on has fallen through the floor.

I'd raise my own right arm, but it's been shattered, fractured. Even my own sword can't save me now.

Whom should I turn to?

Who'll take me in?

Who'll greet me at the door and sweep me in like a long-lost friend?

Who'll appreciate me for what I am, and not compare me with others who've made such progress with such ease?

Only You, Lord God alone, have remained a refuge, a safe house. But in my present distracted state what prevents my bursting in upon You is the damage I've caused You already. I've sinned. Forgive me. Give me a penance, the stiff penance I so rightly deserve. But don't give up on me yet. Of course I know You could abandon me, kick me out, pretend You'd never seen me before — and that'd be okay. In fact, You might just as well hand me over, once and for all, to the Adversary and get it over with!

BUT BEFORE YOU GIVE ME my just desserts, dear Lord, cast Your mind back to the Creation Story, I beg You! Remember how You propped up the collapsed. Now please do the same for me, for You know I can't stand by myself.

That moaning and groaning you hear is my Soul crying out in sadness and loss, in labor and dolor of heart. When my cause comes up before You, don't nihilize, oblivionize, blast me away!

Captivity, incarceration, oppression, exaction — all punishments due to sin, and all punishments due to me. Do look kindly on me, merciful Father. Undo the chain on the prison door and free me from my wretched servitude.

DOES A LONG LIFE make for a better life? In Ecclesiastes, Solomon the Teacher asked the same question (9:1). But who really knows? Living longer just might make for a worse life.

Progress, regress, who knows which direction we're traveling in along the spiritual road? Even Perseverance herself has moments when she doesn't know whether she's coming or going. Why? For a lot of reasons, all having to do with Evils and Devils.

10

Losing the First Fervor

Even after the fire in the refinery, imperfection remains.
(Jeremiah 6:29)

On first conversion many are good and humble. Only later do they become rascally and rebellious. At first blush, they're timorous, atiptoe about everything, respectful, awestruck and devout, mindful of sin and eager for silence. At second blush, however, these very same people've become free and easy, dissolute, chattery, oblivious of the fact that the gate is no longer guarded.

First off they kept the Garden pruned and trimmed. Later they hardly paid attention to what they said or did. Finally, the plot was overrun by Poisonous Orchids and Deadly Nightshade.

Why shouldn't good and modest folk be suspicious and circumspect? With all the bad things happening around them, why shouldn't they feel uncomfortable? I mean, who knows whether he or she has been picked to be one of the Elect? If one did indeed know this precious piece of information, then he or she could put up with all the punishment thrown their way while on earth.

But of course we don't know. That's why everyone has to undergo a trial period, to prove his or her mettle. But who is certain of not being burned by the Fire of Temptation and consumed by the Eternal Flame?

WHAT CAN WE DRAW from these dreadful considerations?

At least two things.

First, everyone ought to be in a continuous state of anxiety about Evil but, also and equally, in a condition of hope when it comes to Good.

Second, no one should presume rashly or be dragged under the bushes by Vain Hope, no matter how trashy she becomes.

Fire turns ore into gold, but corn into ash. Humanity, which do you want to be, gold or husk? Pick one.

The Master Smelter turned up the heat in the furnace and the sons of Levi turned into burning personalities! But as the Dear Jeremiah noted, refining fire doesn't always remove the dross. When the heat cools, gold may be found, but also silver; however, the Lord rejects the silver because it isn't gold. "Rejected silver"—such a terrible term! (29–30).

The prophet Malachi had a somewhat different take. "The Master Smelter will work His fire, refining and purifying the sons of Levi till they've become perfect offerings" (3:3).

LORD GOD, *what joy can I find in the world? When I have to wade through so much uncertainty and infirmity in everything under the sky?*

You, Lord, the Psalmist felt quite certain about because You're so good, because You've been so merciful down the ages to those who had a proper fear of and respect for You (VUL 117:1–4; NRSV 118:1–4).

Your goodness and piety are infinitely greater than all my iniquity. And this'll be my solace, at least as long as You grant me the space and time to make the necessary improvements.

CAPITAL SINS AND
CAPITALIZED NOUNS

Capitalizing the Capital Sins — Pride, Avarice, Lust, Envy, Gluttony, Anger, Sloth — is thought by many editors and copy-editors to be a capital sin, perhaps even a capital crime. But such wisdom as there has been about capitals and capitalization is few and far between.

In 1926, in *A Dictionary of Modern English Usage* by W. H. Fowler, neither "Capitals" nor "Capitalization" were mentioned. In 1965 the second edition appeared, edited by Ernest Gowers; in it there was indeed an entry for "Capitals," but there was precious little help about when to capitalize and when not to. In fact, the prospect was downright gloomy. "Uniformity is lacking not only in practice but also in precept: no two sets of style rules would be found to agree in every respect" (73).

In 1959 and in subsequent editions Strunk and White's *Elements of Style* is silent on the subject.

In 1975, according to the *Harper Dictionary of Contemporary Usage* compiled and edited by William and Mary Morris, "he who takes [capitals] seriously must surely go mad" (107).

In 1982 *The Chicago Manual of Style*, thirteenth edition, revised and expanded since the first edition (1906), offered the following analysis. "In few areas is an author more tempted to overcapitalize or an editor more loath to urge a lowercase style than in that of religion" (208).

Generally held to be the Bible of inerrant style and usage, the *Chicago Manual* went on to offer the following advice. "The editors of the University of Chicago

Press urge a spare, *down* [italics theirs] style in this field as in others: capitalize what are clearly proper nouns and adjectives, and lowercase all else except to avoid ambiguity" (208–209).

"Less is more" — that seems to be the modern wisdom and, as such, I've gladly followed it as an editor and writer for the last forty-five years. So the question arises. Why have I as a modern translator of medieval Latin dotted the landscape of my translation of *Consolations* with capital letters?

Well, Kempis isn't the culprit. His fifteenth-century Latin style seems to have followed the *Chicago Manual's* in spirit and letter, with a capital letter on the first word of each sentence, and not a great deal more.

I'm the culprit. It's my paraphrasal translation of the Latin into modern English that has introduced all the capitals. Yes, it may be a capital sin, even a capital crime, to do so, but I have several very good reasons for doing so.

First, in medieval English prose and poetry, capital letters came quick as dandelions. Divine nouns (God the Father, God the Spirit). Divine pronouns (His and Theirs). Divine Attributes (Omnipotence and Omniscience). Divine Synonyms (Creator, Helper, Savior). Theological Virtues (Faith, Hope, Charity). Capital Sins (Lust, Greed, Sloth). Branches of Knowledge (Theology, Philosophy, Mathematics). And so on. So why not in a modern Englishing of a medieval Latin classic?

Also in medieval English prose and poetry, authors tended not only to capitalize a virtue or vice but also to personify it. As an example may I give the cast of characters of the medieval morality play, *Everyman?* Death, Good Fellowship, Kindred, Cousin, Goods, Good Deeds, Knowledge, Confession, Beauty, Strength, Discretion, and Five Wits. (God, Everyman, Messenger, Angel, and Doctor also have speaking parts.) So why not use such capitalization in a modern translation of Kempis, especially when *Consolations* is a dramatic dialogue?

Capitalization cum Personification, when rendered paraphrasally into modern English, almost always adds clarity to the context but it occasionally produces an astonishing effect. As an example, this paragraph from my Englishing of Kempis's *Imitation.*

"When Virtue strides into the room, Vainglory vanishes. When Heavenly Grace and True Charity sweep into the room, Virid Envy turns up her nose, High Anxiety has a fit, Particular Friendship is beside himself. We all know why. Grace and Charity have this way of clearing the floor of crooks and cranks" (3:9).

Third and last, capitalization is a way of distinguishing what Kempis meant in the fifteenth century from what moderns mean by the same words. In many cases there's a world of difference.

For example, what Kempis meant by "Evil Ones" isn't what the modern world means by "evil ones." The former were, and indeed still are, incredibly vigorous and aggressively hostile creatures from the spiritual world, together with such minions as they've been able to recruit in this world. The latter may mean warm fuzzies, cuddly monsters, with perhaps a few tinpot despots and terrorists thrown in.

What Kempis meant by "Imbeciles" and "Blockheads" isn't what the modern world means by "imbeciles" and "blockheads." Kempis meant a small proud, permanent proprietary group united for a single virtue or vice.

What the modern world means is people who'd wear, if they could, T-shirts emblazoned "Imbeciles and proud of it!" In other words, the moderns mean a state of mind or soul that one can casually slip into and out of from time to time.

As the *Chicago Manual* helped, so it hindered. According to the editors one of the traditional causes of hyperactive capitalization is the "unanalyzed acceptance of the pious custom of an earlier age."

If I may express a contrary opinion, there's nothing ho-hum about a Vice or a Virtue in Kempis's world. Rather it indicates the head-banging, hellzapoppin activity that is characteristic of a healthy spiritual life, then as found in *Consolations*, then in Latin, now in English.

To conclude, two pieces of wisdom from Gowers.

"Let it be repeated: the employment of capitals is a matter not of rules but of taste; but consistency is at least not a mark of bad taste" (75).

Also, according to Gowers, the reader's eye can accommodate to whatever degree of capitalization so long as it's "systematic, logical, and unambiguous" (73).

11

Ranting about the Present Life

How many bad days do I have left?

(Psalm VUL 101:24; NRSV 102:23.)

As long as I have a foot in this world, dear Reader, I'm a mess, a complete mess.

As long as I remain here, I'm just a poor pilgrim, a mere hanger-on at the many holy spots around the world — the Letter to the Hebrews has said much the same thing (11:13).

I hauled nothing into this world, and nothing's what I'm going to cart out. Paul said much the same in his First to Timothy (6:7).

Without a stitch I arrived, and without a stitch I'll depart; that was Job's experience (1:21).

Like a shadow moving across a landscape — that's how the Book of Wisdom put it (5:9).

A feather riding the wind.

One-night stands at the hostelries of the world followed the next morning by on-the-road agains.

That's all the present life is, a very brief night. Head on a hard pillow for only a few moments, then off again.

My days are few, and they're hard, hard as nails, as Jacob said to the Pharaoh in Genesis (47:9). And after a modest life, I'll have used them all up. I'll have passed over the water and caused not a ripple.

Dead as a doornail; cheap as a tintype.

Who'll do the honors with my ripe cadaver?

Why would we take notice of the dead-and-gone when he never amounted to anything while he was alive and well?

HUMAN MEMORY IS SHORT — in this the more famous fare no better than the less famous — but eternal memory is long. God doesn't die, and God doesn't forget. Or so it delighted the Psalmist to remind us (VUL 111:7; NRSV 112:7).

Therefore, dear Reader, happy the devout who doesn't put his hope in Humanity, who doesn't take excessive pleasure in worldliness. He's already hung his heart in Heaven — he knows his whole earthly caboodle is kaput.

INVENTORY ALL the earthly things from the beginning of the world right up to now, dear Reader, and then tell me what they amount to.

Look around and ask all the people you meet how long they think they're going to last.

The only answer to this informal survey, or so the Psalmist would have us believe, is that everyone and everything don't amount to a hill of beans and that everything is vanity, puffery, an eclair without an éclat, a now-you-see-it — now-you-don't (VUL 38:6; NRSV 39:6).

What a pathetic, preposterous life this is! Laughable and yet, at the same time, lamentable! The sort of life Good People endure rather than enjoy. As for Bad People, they think that this is the only life, but in the end they too have to let go.

Vanity is a runaway, with no end or stop or destination. Where will you come to a stop?

But the time will come, or so Paul wrote to his Romans, when all the Elect will be freed from the servitude of corruption (8:21). When they were on earth, they were antsy about taking the next step, even though they knew they were a long way from the kingdom of Christ.

Would that this whole world would turn, dear Reader, into prawns, not prunes!

Would that my all and plenty would be the sweet Lord God Himself, my immortal spouse!

It's the bitterest cup, all the racing around in this life!

Let them drink if they want because everyone pays the inevitable price in the end. The drunker one becomes, the sharper pain feels. Why is that? It should be the other way around. That's because all the jocund things in life are jokes. They're gone with the wine, leaving behind only lees, dregs, sediment — all spit-outs for the spittoons.

What's a serious person to conclude?

I'm not a serious person myself, but what am I to conclude?

Flee from me, False Glory of the world! And take with you every empty and carnal joy! You tempt many and drag them under the bushes, but in the end you'll abandon them, leaving them to die of their own disease.

Alas to those who believed in all the foolishness! Woe to you who brought all the foolishness!

Dear friends on the pilgrimage road — Humility and her jolly friend Derision, exposer of all the pomps and poops of the world, and Remembrance. Good companions all on the pilgrimage road. For our mutual protection, let's stick together!

12

Unpacking My Bag
for the Final Trip

Sad is my Soul on the way to Death!
(Matthew 26:38)

What am I, dear Reader, but a cinder, a mere ember of my once and future life? Where else am I headed but to the dustbin of existence?

O how wretched I've become! No wonder I weep, making my rounds as a pilgrim and yet ignoring the end I'm sure to come to.

BUT IF I SHALL HAVE lived well, dear Reader, persevered to the end, then there's no great need to fear a bad death. Your good life and a clear conscience should help, although one doesn't want to get caught swanning about proclaiming the wonderfulness of his or her own spiritual life. Be proud about God, yes, but feel sad about sin. Even so, living becomes less tolerable with every passing day. And yet the Prophet, full of trepidation, was able to speak without trepidation.

"My heart's packed and ready, O God," sighed the Psalmist; "my heart's prepared to go" (VUL 107:2; NRSV 108:1).

Lord God of my salvation, give me a good end to my life, and don't prolong the days of my suffering.

Wailing I came into this prison of life, and wailing I'll depart.

FREQUENT VISITATIONS by Misery and Sadness make this life seem long to me. And yet the days, swifter than runners, race around the course with ever-increasing speed (Job 9:25).

For the person who's harassed by Sadness and Pain, each day drags on as though it were a year.

As for me this life is slow, boring, tedious. Misery and Sadness come to commiserate and then, poor girls, they forget to leave.

IF PERCHANCE some joys and jewels of consolations rear their jolly heads, do examine them closely. They may come from God, or they may not. If from God, do welcome them warmly. Even if they don't last long, they're still nice to have. But what I really wish were longer, dear Lord, is Your visits. They're all too short.

However, if these consolations aren't from God but seem to have happy faces, they can be nice too. But more often than not, they're vile, despicable, destructive. That's what life's all about, good and bad mixing together, sometimes hard to tell apart.

WHAT CAN ONE CONCLUDE?

As long as I'm here on earth, dear Reader, I'm a pauper, a pilgrim. I can't say I've ever had enough; there's no such thing as *enough* in the present life. But there's one good I do expect, Lord, and it's You in whom I believe.

When therefore Your glory appears and has filled me to the brim, I'll cry out with the Psalmist! (VUL 16:15; NRSV 17:15).

In the meantime my Soul continues to thrash about. "Sad is my Soul all the way to death." That's what You cried out in the garden of Gethsemane, Lord, and I know what You meant (Matthew, 26:38). In the meantime, before my sorrowing and suffering have flown this earthly coop, all I have, all I cling to, is You, Your piety, Your faithfulness. Lord — You're my only protection.

DEVOTIO MODERNA

Devotio Moderna was a reform movement, a renewal movement, a good example of *ecclesia semper refor-manda,* a church always renewing itself, the sort of activity that keeps an old entity from becoming an odd entity. Simply put, the reformers felt that the Church had lost touch with the people.

The Modern Devotion, as it was called in English, peaked in the fifteenth century and in the sixteenth century piqued the next wave of reformers who, some of them anyway, destroyed the Brethren and Sistern of the Common Life. The levelers too felt that the Church had lost touch with the people.

With its roots in the Netherlands, the Modern Devotion spread over much of northern Europe. One hundred houses of the Brethren rose, and three hundred houses of the Sistern. By virtue of the international traffic in manuscripts, especially from one monastery to another, the Modern Devotion spread even farther. In England it quickly came to be thought that the *Imitation* had been written by the author of such thoroughly English works as *The Ladder of Perfection* and *The Cloud of Unknowing.*

From the first short chapter of the First Book (there are four) of the *Imitation,* one can immediately gather the drift of the work and indeed the movement.

SPIRIT OF PURSUIT

"'The Devout who shadows my every move won't lose me in the dark.' At least that's what Christ says, or what the Evangelist John says Christ said (8:12). He tells us to walk on, through the darkness, with Christ as our only torch. That way, when morning comes, we mayn't have gained a step, but we won't have lost one either. And on into the day we must pursue with doggéd tread the life of Jesus Christ."

SPIRIT OF CHRIST

"We Devouts know more about Christ than we do about the Saints. For example, the Devout who finds the spirit of Christ discovers in the process many 'unexpected delights,' if I may use an expression of the Apostle John's from the last book of the New Testament (2:17).

"But that isn't often the case. Many who've heard the Gospel over and over again think they know it all. They've little desire to discover if there's more to the story. That's because, as the Apostle Paul diagnosed it in his letter to the Romans (8:9), 'they don't have the spirit of Christ.'

"On the other hand, the Devout who wants to understand the words of Christ fully and slowly savor their sweetness has to work hard at making himself another Christ."

VANITY OF THE KNOWABLES

"If you're not humble, you make the Trinity nervous, and in that wretched state, what possible good do you get out of standing up in public and disputing to high heaven about the Trinity as an intellectual entity? The real truth, if only you'd learn it, is that hifalutin words don't make a Devout a saint. Only a virtuous life can do that, and only that can make God care for us.

"Compunction is a good example. The Schoolmen at the University could produce lengthy, perhaps even lacy, definitions of this holy word, but that wouldn't move them one inch closer to the Gate of Heaven. The humble Devout, on the other hand, who can neither read nor write, might very well have experienced compunction every day of his life; he's the one, whether he knows it or not, who'll find himself already waiting at that very gate when the Final Day comes.

"Are you any the richer, if I may put it the way Paul did in his First to the Corinthians (13:3), for knowing all the proverbs of the Bible and all the axioms of the Philosophers, when you're really all the poorer for not knowing the charity and the grace of God?

"'Vanity of vanities, and everything is vanity,' says the Ancient Hebrew Preacher (Ecclesiastes 1:2). The only thing that isn't vanity is loving God and, as Moses preached to the Israelites, serving him alone (Deuteronomy 6:13). That's the highest wisdom, to navigate one's course, using the contempt of the world as a chart, toward that heavenly port."

VANITY OF THE PERISHABLES

"Just what is vanity? Well, it's many things. A portfolio of assets that are bound to crash. A bird-breast of medals and decorations. A brassy solo before an unhearing crowd. The alley-catting one's 'carnal desires,' as Paul so lustily put it to the Galatians (5:16), only to discover that punishment awaits further up and farther in. Pining for a long life and at the same time paying no attention to the good life. Focusing both eyes on the present without casting an eye toward the future. Marching smartly in the passing parade instead of falling all over oneself trying to get back to that reviewing stand where Eternal Joy is queen."

VANITY OF THE VISIBLES

"Don't forget the hoary wisdom of the Ancient Hebrew Preacher. 'The eye is never satisfied by what it sees; nor the ears, by what they hear' (Ecclesiastes 1:8). With that in mind, try to transfer your holdings from the visible market into the invisible one. The reason? Those who trade in their own sensualities only muck up their own account and in the process muddy up God's Final Account."

—Thomas à Kempis, *The Imitation of Christ,* translated by William Griffin (San Francisco: HarperSanFrancisco, 2000), 3–5.

A caution. Kempis, and indeed the Modern Devotion, has traditionally been thought of as anti-intellectual. But that's far from the truth. Kempis himself was something of an intellectual.

Two points. First, university men, even while dealing with divine topics, often sailed off into the fairyland of the intellect. Second, Systematic Theology wasn't all in the books, except, of course, in the books of the Bible and books of Ascetical Theology (another name for Christian spirituality).

As a historical movement *Devotio Moderna* may have passed away but, through the writings of Kempis and his fellows, especially the *Imitation of Christ,* it has become a *devotio perennis;* that's to say, a devotion for all times, but especially ours. – W.G.

13

Panting for Eternal Life

Show my Soul the way out of prison!
(Psalm VUL 141:8; NRSV 142:7)

The pain is killing me, Lord!
  I can't put up with it any more!
  Why would I want to hang around here?
  I don't know how I can keep my strength up.
  Yes, I inch along in the spiritual life, but it's entirely too slow for my taste. Such prayer that I offer — if indeed it is a prayer — is that I don't lose today what little ground I gained yesterday.

YOU'D DO a good thing for me, Lord, if You'd whisk me out of here before things get any worse!
  Pain in, pain out — that's how I breathe. Work provides little distraction.
  Under the fire of my repeated requests, Lord, nothing! You call it Patience. I call it Abuse.
  You could, of course, smooth things out a little. I'd suffer still, but perhaps not so much as before.

SO WHY DON'T YOU take Your humble servant out of here, Lord? Why does he have to stand on this one spot and not move a muscle? Why does he have to sit in a corner and think of the color white? Why does he have to live with Good People? They should improve his manners and his morals, but they don't.

Why does he spend so much time conversing with his betters? He's such a slicker and slacker.

Sad thing, this, to have to pour my pathetic prayers directly into Your ear trumpet, O God — but don't You dare return the favor! I don't want You pouring Your distresses back into my small ears. Have Your Angels, if You must, fell the tree and feed the wood to the fire!

Yes, I acknowledge my infirmity right in front of You, Lord, much as it pains me. And I'll continue to do so until You say, *Enough's enough!*

MINE IS TO POINT the finger at myself. Yours is to point the finger at Yourself.

Mine is to weep, tear my clothes, and carry on as though I were really sorry for what I've done. Yours is to console the poor weeping sot as though he were totally sincere.

Either / Or, Lord God.

Either You keep me on this earth and give me the necessary grace to carry it out, *Or* You sweep me off this earth before the chasm between this world and the next grows still farther apart! Why? To live a long life in this world and not grow better is only to accumulate more punishment in the next. A life that knows no progress has no appeal for me.

The person who lives holily and justly has to wade through defects that are hip high in order that he might increase in Virtue and Grace. That's to say, he must keep himself in a state of never-ending distaste for this world and never-dying desire for the next.

WHAT WILL A PERSON here on earth — already a victim of low self-esteem — do when, against every movement of the Spirit, he feels his flesh surge?

SOME PERSONS are never overcome with the tedium of *Te Deum* and never succumb to the numbness of tepidity. They're always in battle gear ready to fight to the death with the Flesh. They're the sort of people who approach the death of the Body at a run. The people who live the life of the flesh, on the other hand, dressed only in their draws, run right smack into the death of the Soul right on their own hearth rug.

WHEN SEDUCTION and her evil twin Simulation (of the Friend by the Enemy) come a-knocking, bar the door.

No one's totally secure. No one's entirely without blame. Alas, Fragility — who let that old tart in? — has done everybody in the room at least twice.

LORD, I KNOW You do everything and know everything — yes, I'm buttering You up for a favor — will You repair my broken heart, clean my sordid Soul? Will You put new spirit in my veins?

Once upon a time Tepidity and Apathy, mad sisters both, made a slow but grand entrance into my life. Would You kindly encourage them to make a fast exit? Will you welcome back Spiritual Fervor, the prodigal who's just returned? Will you match me step by step on the rest of my bloody pilgrimage?

14

Slipsliding through Life

The torch of Hell awaits Slipsliders.
(Job 12:5)

As if I had to tell You, Lord, I'm the sort of person who trips himself up as a matter of course. I'm my own best foul-up. It's the weight I carry that does me in every time; that's to say, the terrible weight of my own sins. Grant me the Grace, and the weight will melt away.

You know that already, Lord, but just in case You don't, this is the Grace I pray for. Without it there can't be such a thing as the "Good Life." Nor can there be, for that matter, "Eternal Life."

As LONG AS I traipse about in this baggy ill-fitting body, Consolation seems to avoid me. Who can imagine a worse situation? Really, Death is better than a life like this.

Why is that?

Because life on this earth is just a very poor preparation for Eternal Life. Which can't come until and unless Death does the Present Life in. And in the act Death itself is destroyed. Well, I must say, Lord, You could've arranged things better!

AND SO DESIRE has come back to visit me again. And my heart seeking Eternal Rest breathes heavily, cries out loudly.

Enough to make me happy, Lord, would be for You to carry my Soul off, right now, this very same Soul you've already washed, bathed, cleansed in Your holy Blood.

Open the gate of Your Kingdom and let the Pauperous Pilgrim pass through, the long-lost pilgrim returning from his ragged exile.

Hear me, Lord, and let me return my corporeal costume!

What more can I do on earth? I'm useless to myself and of no use to others.

WHAT'S THE USE of going on living? For me it's just another day carrying my load uphill. For the others it's just another day of tedium, boredom, ennui.

What's to become of me, Lord? I haven't the foggiest. If You'd provided better for me, my desires wouldn't be getting in my way. After all, You do have my consent form to do everything You want to me.

WHENEVER I REVIEW my record, Lord, I find only bad. Why must living in this world be my burden and my boredom?

Today I sin. I heap sin onto sin. And as convenient as it is to confess, I don't.

If only I could escape from this body that has brought me only to sin and join You in the Kingdom, then I'd never sin again. I'd be done sinning for the rest of eternity. That would mean that You'd stop being offended, and start being praised, by every little thing I do or don't do.

Up to now You've sustained me, Lord, but just barely. You've shown me every patience, if I may put the kindest spin on Your behavior toward me.

Funny thing, though; I know my faults. They're no strangers to me. It's because of them that I haven't been able to enter the Kingdom before now. Nothing nasty, nothing unclean in the Kingdom!

When I'm finally found without sin, I can only imagine that I'll be sponged from top to bottom. I won't be afraid then; at least, not of being turned away at the door. Rather I'll be looking forward to passing right through the solid door, won't I?

If I don't progress more fervently and if I don't pay more attention to the whole task, I fear that what pathetic little hope I have left won't be enough of a ticket to get in.

Lord, You're in the business of saving Souls, I know that, and You'd take no pleasure in a Soul that's not making the grade. So bestow on me more grace, or at least enough grace, to turn my life around. And in the hope of celestial goods, grant me the spirit of internal richness.

Some wishes.

May my heart never dance to the tune of the flesh!

May no creature or worldly care get in my way!

May You, the object of my desire, continue to attract me and console me.

Blessed is the person who waits on the Lord.

More blessed is the person who's already taken leave of this world—he's the one who's left all evil behind.

15

Sighing for the Final Hour

Ever since I can remember, Lord, You've been my only hope.
(Psalm VUL 70:5; NRSV 71:5.)

In the hope of obtaining Grace I fly to You, Lord and Friend, as the Final Hour fast approaches. If I'd prepared well for this moment, then I could've died in the arms of Grace! If only I could've brought this day to a close with a happy transit and deposited my lousy load on the other side, I could have avoided these last-minute anxieties.

"Happy the person You've chosen and helped to Heaven," sighed the Psalmist (VUL 64:5; NRSV 65:4). His body's been buried, and his Soul's already passed from this world to the Father! From exile to kingdom! From prison to palace! From darkness to light! From death to life! From danger to security! From labor to rest! And from all the worldly miseries to Perpetual Beatitude!

HAPPY THE SOUL who's claimed his reward, rejoicing in You, my Lord, my God! "But alas," if I may borrow a few words from the Psalmist, "my earthly sentence has been prolonged out of all proportion!" (VUL 119:5; NRSV 120, 6).

How graceful and merciful You would've been to me, Lord, if only You'd invited me sooner, instead of perpetually postponing it the way You do!

IF MY TAKING OFF from this world had only been sooner, I would've left my sordid baggage behind long ago. And to think I used to break out in hives at the very thought of committing a sin, at the very same time You were bestowing on me such good stuff.

Yes, I've lived longer than I hoped, but that has only served to make the distance between You and me farther. How? By my committing a bundle of sins in the meantime!

What a botch I've made of it. I've followed all the fleshy stuff! I've fallen for all the flashy stuff! I've given the virtuous life the slip. I've left my innocence exposed. In other words, I've become expert where I should have remained inexpert. Yes, as the prophet Isaiah spat out, "Spit on me, Lord, for all my improprieties" (3:11).

It took me a while to return to my senses. I began slowly. I dawdled along the way. I haven't really rekindled my first fervor. In fact, I've doused it forever, snuffed it out for good.

I suppose that's why I've so often feared death; I just haven't lived as I ought, as my conscience urged me to do.

And yet, even as my sins kept getting worse, my desire of death kept getting stronger.

THE PRAYER I'M TALKING ABOUT went something like this.

Lord, if I were to die in Grace now, I'd no longer be afflicted with the evils of the earth. If You were to harvest my Soul in the near future, You'd put an end, a very fine end, to a very sad life.

WHO WAS KEMPIS?

He was himself, of course, but in time he acquired several other selves.

Thomas Haemerken was born in 1379 or 1370 in Kempen, a village near Düsseldorf in what was then the Rhineland. His father was a blacksmith, and his mother something of a schoolmistress.

In 1393, following in his older brother's footsteps, he left his country home and went to the city of Deventer. For a while he stayed at the house of Florent Radewijns, who eventually took the young man under his wing and indeed under his roof.

There Thomas might have met Gerard Groote, founder of a small faith community called, for want of a better name, Brothers of the Common Life. It was a ragtag crowd, made up mostly of lay people who wanted more, much more, of everything spiritual than they were able to get in their local churches.

Some of the regulars — perhaps I should say "irregulars" since "regulars" meant those already vowed to a religious rule or ruler, like a bishop — had jobs and families and came at night for the spiritual refreshment. Others lived in the house, kept their day jobs, contributed to a common purse. Odd thing, though. No vows or promises; no attempt to formalize this loosey-goosey group into a religious community under the protection and indeed inspection of the local bishop.

In 1399 Thomas moved uphill to the monastery of St. Agnes where there was a community of Augustinians. There he entered the religious order, where his brother John à Kempis was now prior. He was ordained there in 1431 and died there in 1471.

But long before his death Thomas found himself at the gate of Heaven. That's to say, at the doorway to the scriptorium where the Augustinians earned enough income to survive by copying manuscripts, sacred as well as profane. In this happy room, amid pots of inks and piles of writing materials, was a whole publishing enterprise. In it Kempis was said to have copied, among many other works, the Latin Vulgate Bible of St. Jerome — four times.

As for the Brothers and indeed the Sisters of the Common Life downhill, he never really left them. That's to say, he serviced them as well as his own community as spiritual director, novice master, subprior. Most of his life, however, he spent in the writing room cum library — and that's where he assumed at least two additional identities.

Thomas archived the works of Groote and Radewijns and others, however loosely connected with the group. He used their materials for his own edification first and then for the edification of others. That's to say, he ordered their works, edited them, took extracts from them for inclusion in anthologies like *Imitation* and *Consolations*.

The *Imitation* was widely circulated before someone thought to put Kempis's name on the title page. Apparently, he didn't complain. But when one speaks of Thomas Haemerken as an author, one includes Groote and Radewijns and perhaps others, whether one knows it or not. —W.G.

16

Lusting for the Last Breath

My earthly sentence has been prolonged out of all proportion!
(Psalm VUL 119:5; NRSV 120, 6)

True it is, Lord, that everything is in Your good care. True it is also that if I do what You want me to do, things will rattle along rather nicely. But if I don't do as You say, then do Your worst.

I can worm my desire into Your presence, Lord, without Your even knowing it. And when You do find out, I can endure your huffing and puffing. For my excuse I'll just say that I had no prior knowledge of the naughtiness I'd just caused. Of course, if my excuse misfires, I'll have no recourse. I'll just put on my woolly cap and mittens and wait for You to turn my heavenly residence into an icehouse.

Well, Lord, I know I'm not well enough prepared yet. My weighty conscience tells me that. And the Early Fathers tell me that also. They were sinners too, and they often took one road when You'd advised them to take another.

How SHOULD I prepare myself? I ask for the thousandth time, and for the thousandth time I know the answer.

First, I shouldn't care a fig if the Last Day is today or tomorrow.

Second, I should renew my will, deplore my past negligences, burn up the track wholly for you, and commit myself to Your mercy forever.

MY LORD AND MY GOD, *may all my pomps and poops stand down in Your mercy. None of them have any merit of their own unless Your piety is present. As we all know, Your capacity is immense. No hoopla on my part — just a little hope.*

SO MUCH FOR THE LAGGARD SOUL. What does the chaste and devout Soul have to say? Probably some sentiments from Hebrews.

Come, Lord Jesus, come. Don't dawdle! Quiet my hysterics. Unleash my shackles from the confines of prison. Lead me from the wallow of misery and the mire of the outhouse (10:13, 19, 22).

WAITING? I've done nothing but wait for You to hear my case!

Don't leave me any longer, piddling and puddling about this age of mine. I've battled enough. I've lived as an exile long enough. I'd enjoy Your company even if I don't deserve it. That's why I want You to look into my case, even though I can't look You in the eye.

I want to enjoy the long-hoped-for Joy that searches for an end that has no end, and isn't shrouded with the pall of tedium, ennui, boredom.

Show me the face Your Angels see. Let me hear the voice Your Angels hear. Let's stop this Hide-and-Seek, Bride-and-Groom, Song-of-Songs sort of chase.

Come, Lord Jesus, and rescue me from this alien land. Summon this pitiful servant home. Repair this lapse in my service to You. Come, Good Redeemer; add me to those who've already participated in Your eternal glory. It's time that I return to You again. It's time to commend me to the earth, which is my body's true home.

IT DOESN'T MATTER how my corpse is handled or where it's finally stashed. Wherever, it won't be remote or unknown to You, my Lord and Friend. My spirit survives, still very much alive, and is scheduled to arrive at Your manse shortly before dawn.

May my spirit fare well when I commend it to You. Don't think too harshly on my flesh, for it too will rise on the Last Day to join me in enjoying Your presence.

PLUCK ME FROM THE CROWD and introduce me to the society of Your Saints. Why now? Because as Job once said, "Life on this earth is such a grind, such a trudge" (10:1). The only thing that delights me now is the thought of life in Heaven.

THE THOUGHT OF DEATH doesn't upset me mightily. Your Holy Angels are Your faithful assistants in this regard. As I die wearily, may they protect me virily! May they pick me up gently and leniently! May they lead me in appropriate, if humble, procession to the heavenly Paradise.

May the glorious mother of God, the Virgin Mary, assist as well as the rest of the whole Heavenly Crowd.

And You, good Jesus and sweet, turn Your face to me at last. Don't single me out as the only reprobate in Your holy sainted crowd. Set them straight, Son of God, that You redeemed me from the Enemy by means of Your precious blood. Raise me up in Your Glory, Mercy, Goodness. Why? As You were caught saying in Luke's Gospel, "With desire I've desired it, desired to spend Easter eastering with You" (22:15).

Happy day, the Day of Reward I've desired for so long!

Blessed hour, the hour I pass over!

Long have I desired this, and long have I kept the goal before my eyes!

The tribulations and pressures of this world have left their marks on me. But hard work and humiliation on behalf of Your name were the killers.

To live for You used to mean everything; now to die for You is the only thing — so Paul wrote to his Philippians (1:21). Much better still is to finally be at home with You in the kingdom of Heaven.

May Glory and Praise be Yours, O Life of the Living and Hope of the Dying!

May they be the Salvation and Rest of all who arrive there!

17

Dying on This Side of the Grave

Shade my eyes from Vanity's blinding flash!
(Psalm VUL 118:37; NRSV 119:37.)

O Jesus, True Life, Life that knows not Death, a prayer.

I don't mind being roughed up by Love, wounded by Love, crucified for Love. Anything but letting my flimsy Flesh hug me to death.

Yes, Lord, I'm dead to the world. Or perhaps more accurately, I'm all but dead to the world. Even at this late date in my life, the Old Man of the Scriptures lives in me, brawling, wrangling, raising Cain, making my nights so drawn out and my days so draggy!

WHEN WILL IT HAPPEN, dear Reader, that I may say with some assurance, perhaps even with some pride, "I'm conducting myself as though I were dead even though I'm still on this side of the grave"?

I CAN'T BELIEVE I just said that, and I have no idea what it means!

I suppose it means not caring a hoot for credits and plaudits. I suppose it means not caring a fig for blamers and accusers. I suppose it means being dead to the world.

By way of contrast, the person who's dead in the flesh has no sense of smell, can't taste a thing, doesn't break a sweat. Nor does he hear the top twenty pops or see the passing parade or wear bright shiny beads.

By way of comparison, the person's who's said to be dead to the world is actually alive in God. As Paul wrote to his Colossians, "You're dead, dead as dodoes, to all intents and purposes; your real life is with Christ in God" (3:3).

As Paul spoke, so he thought, seeing exteriors as though they were interiors. How? Because what's on the outside's a piddle, and what's in the inside flows eternal.

Actually, Paul cast a rather longer view, and it was that vista that excited him. Toward this he set his heart. This he wished, this he loved, this he sought, this he could taste in his mouth — what lay hidden inside. That's to say, the Great Good, the Greatest Good of All, the Eternal Good, about whom there's never enough time to think. That's because the Lord's the Good Person who's too dear, too sweet, too delectable, but not all that effable!

Why is the Lord so aloof from us, I mean, what with His well-known proclivity for parties?

Odd thing, that! Parties revel in externals, enjoy delectables; concentrate on the here-and-now, postpone the once-and-future; flee the bitter and shun the rough. All of which, or so He's told us Himself, are often considered quite healthy to the spirit. That's not to say the spirit's allowed to trample through the tulips without actually pausing to trumpet their beauty.

THE PERSON WHO has the grace of Spiritual Fortitude has the edge when it comes to subjugating the insolent movements of the Flesh. You'll know that person when you meet him; he's always troubadouring the word of Divine Virtue.

"Even though the Flesh eats me alive," cried the Psalmist, "the Lord will keep me alive" (vul 117:6; nrsv 118:6).

Sensuality incites war, and Flesh incites revolution, but the Spiritual Person doesn't easily give his assent. The principle seems to be, though, the greater the love of God, the more interior the comfort He gives.

Whenever the Soul is drawn to God so sweetly, so forcefully, so ardently, it's rapt and held senseless. That's to say, it doesn't see the stuff that's around it, the sort of stuff that cries, "Wolf!" That's because the Lord's there and not there at one and the same time. The Soul's not in the stuff, it's above the stuff, in God and with God, who makes His presence known interiorly, raises the Soul up, and sends it off on a toot, as if in a chariot of fire. That's how the Soul enjoyed Him in person before it had to entertain Him in desire.

18

Distancing from Creatures

Yes, I've fled a long flight and, yes,
I've come to rest on a rocky point.

(Psalm VUL 54:8; NRSV 55:7)

How nice to find a quiet place to roost! What a relief not to have to talk up a storm! How sweet it is to talk with God and not use words! Words without noise, noise without words — that's the way it is with God!

How nice to enjoy a one-on-one with the One-and-Only, the *Summum Bonum,* the Bundle of all Bonums, the Boodle of all Bundles!

Would that I were in the Inner Room with the Simple and the Singular. Then I'd never be distracted by the passing parade. Nor would I let my eyes linger upon the passing paraders.

"To LIBERATE MY SOUL from my Body I want to die," wrote the Apostle Paul rather jauntily to the Romans. "Why would I want to do that? Because then I'd be the happiest man alive!" (7:24).

Well, I don't know about Paul, but I haven't died once, not yet anyway. Yes, my Soul has often died, done in by the very creatures it came to love. That happens, but how can it happen over and over again? Well, my poor Soul forgets, but also perhaps what attracts me most to a creature may just be its reflection, some small glint, of the Creator who made the creature in the first place.

My MIND just can't make up its mind, wishing one thing, then another; seeking peace in creatures and not finding it.

Every creature has a glamour, every created thing a glitter. A creature is most happy when it's being used. What creature would ever say, "I'm good, yes, I'm very good, but please don't pick me up, please don't stare at me as though you can't live without me"? Not one!

"WHO CAN UNDERSTAND such a thing?" Doesn't that just sound like Jeremiah confronting yet another conundrum (17:9). But You, God, You know how the mind works, what makes it tick; are creatures just cloud puff balls? So asked the Psalmist some centuries ago (VUL 93:11; NRSV 94:11). But I'm a creature of Yours, Lord, God, Governor of all You survey. Am I just a cloud puff ball? I thought I was made to love You, and now I want to love You, but I find I can't love You as much as I'd like.

LITTLE DO WE CREATURES KNOW, dear Reader, that Humankind has sticky fingers and hence can't easily put down what it casually picks up. Of course, I've tried, but I know I must look absolutely silly trying to separate myself from created things. Finally, thankfully, there came a time when I thought I'd left them behind forever.

But had I? As I made my final exit from creaturedom, I looked behind and there they were, following me, all the creatures and created things in my life, like pigeons in a park, fully confident, fully expectant. Of course I could get rid of them. All I had to do was clap my hands. That set them off on a tear, and then they were back. Another clap, and another, and another until the blood in my fingers ran! Apparently, alas, there's no way on this earth to rid oneself of creatures once and for all.

IN THE MEANTIME, Dear Lord, I saw, by virtue of intuition, what had been invisible to me up to now. That's to say, You as the *Summum Bonum*. Well, I must say, You *seemed* to take some delight in my presence but then, suddenly, without notice, You swept me from Your Presence. Why? Something about some dumb thing I'd done, and then I was worse off than ever before.

What God said to Noah and his sons in Genesis (9:12), I feel I should say to You now. It's time I made some sort of solemn pledge or vow. You're the only one I want to know and love. I don't care what the others do. All I want is to close my eyes to everything, turn my pockets inside out, swallow myself whole and entire.

EVEN AFTER DOING ALL THIS, there still remains my friendly, next-door neighbor, an admired and yet admitted sinner. He always has a smile on his face and a friendly slap on my back, and he's always trying to interest me in the latest gidgets and gadgets, suggesting all the time how much they'd improve the quality of my daily life. But what he hides behind his grin is his grimace; that's to say, his bad breath, his hard heart, his nagging desire to drag me under the bushes.

IN CONCLUSION, Lord, every time You felt I'd come too close to creatures and created things, You distanced Yourself from me in a flash. That's when I knew how truly delinquent I'd been! I should've stuck with all the firm purposes of amendment I made on Your behalf. What a pity! I was made to love You and enjoy Your presence but, somehow, creatures and other created things, those rascally rabbits in Your lovely garden, found me such an easy mark. Rescue me, Dear Lord, and set me on the well-manicured path. Don't let me dally among the annuals. It's the perennials I want to admire.

WHO OWNS KEMPIS?

At least one good thing came out of the Reformation and Counter-Reformation. Both sides — Luther and Loyola — claimed Kempis as their exclusive possession. Fortunately, he didn't have to choose sides, what with his having died some hundred years before the Wittenberg Door. Today, Catholics, Protestants, and Evangelicals alike know Kempis as author of *The Imitation of Christ*, a guide for the Christian pilgrimage.

He lived in the fifteenth century, a time when Catholicism flourished. There wasn't a great deal to be ecumenical about then. Protestantism and Evangelicalism had yet to come down the pike. But in the twenty-first century we would call some passages of his pure ecumenism.

As an illustration, I pick some paragraphs from the fourth book of the *Imitation*. Dealing as it does with the Blessed Sacrament, they haven't been read by most Protestant and Evangelicals, but they have a striking ecumenical appeal.

"My body's a prison, and the view from my cell is grim. I survive, but barely. I do without things in this wretched state, but two things I just can't live without. Food and Light. And You, dear Lord, You bring them to me in the middle of the night.

"Food? Your Sacred Body, which revives my sagging mind and body.

"Light? Your Divine Word. As the Psalmist has sung in similar circumstances, it's a lamp for my shackled feet" (119, 105).

"Without the Food and without the Light I wither. Without the Bread and without the Bible I wander. Without the Sacrament of Life and the Book of Life, I perish.

"From my cell I see — or think I see — an altar. A Holy Table from which rises Holy Church in all her splendor. On one side is the Holy Bread, that's to say, the precious Body of Christ. On the other, the Holy Bible; that's to say, the Divine Law that contains Holy Doctrine, teaches right faith, leads even the imprisoned soul through the veil of veils to the Holy of Holies, as the Letter to the Hebrews has led us to expect" (6, 19).

—Thomas à Kempis, *The Imitation of Christ,* translated by William Griffin (San Francisco: HarperSanFrancisco, 2000), 257.

Food and Light, Bread and Bible, Body of Christ and Holy Bible — Kempis said he couldn't live without both to sustain him. And we, Christians of every stripe, would do well to follow his example.

In addition to remembering the *Imitation,* Catholics, Protestants, and Evangelicals may now remember Kempis for his *Consolations.* —W.G.

19

Condemning Earthly Consolations

There's plenty of earthly consolation around,
but my Soul will have none of it.

(Psalm VUL 76:3; NRSV 77:2)

Don't wander off, my Soul, in search of baubles and bangles on the grounds that they're the consolations you've been looking for. Just find your way back to the Lord — He's the font of all Consolation.

Whatever it is you're seeking in creatures and created things, you should pound with a great pestle until you turn it into damp and dust! Such solace is momentary, just a tickle on the tum, a tingle on the lip, a pinch on the cheek, a chuck under the chin. If anything, you should really demand rather more of creatures. Such a shame that they never deliver.

Why should this bit of news upset you?

IT MAKES NO SENSE to beg from a beggar. Every creature is a beggar where Consolation's concerned. On the other hand, as the Letter of James reminds us (1:5), God is rich in grace, and He doesn't mind if we hit Him up for some loose change every once in a while. In fact, He has seemingly bottomless pockets, and never tires of hearing our dreary tales for the umpteenth time. All one has to do is find out where He is on any given day and get in the queue.

"FLOWN THE COOP, my Soul? Return at once," as the Genesist might say (8:9). "Return as the dove returned to Noah in the Ark," to Christ in my heart's secret place.

SAY NO to exterior consolation when it's offered to you. It's hard at first, but it gets easier as you go on.

Don't be crazy like that crow who flew off from the Ark, only to come back before he found consolation. Be more like the racing pigeon, fleeing quickly even as it's yearning to return. That's to say, may Christ feed you with the Bread of Heaven whenever you feel the yearn for it.

EVEN IF NECESSITY or infirmity dogs your tracks, dear Soul, avoid further delay. Return as quickly as you can lest you drown in the flood of words one hears abroad, lest you be snared by the Enemy on the prowl.

Many are the snares for the Soul wandering where it will. Hence, the quicker the dove returns, the greater the chance his feathers will be intact.

Conclusion? You, my devout Soul, should fly back to your cell and seriously consider how dangerous it is to be anywhere else.

BLESSED, THE SOUL who's not afraid to show his linen to the Lord, no earthly joy hidden in its folds, no earthly hatred staining its sheets.

Blessed, the Soul who doesn't squeeze the living daylights out of creatures but puts all hope into the Consolation of Consolations.

Blessed, the Soul who rejects the Flesh and the Flash on earth and freely embraces the Trek and the Trudge for Christ.

Blessed, the Soul who in the Great Search doesn't find its own glory and never desires its own will be done, but rather preaches the glory of God in all things.

Blessed, the Soul who alienates itself from all temporal things and in all its actions purifies itself for the presence of God.

Blessed, the Soul whose desires are raised on high, whose arms are outstretched like the Cherub's wings in Ezechiel (NRSV Ezekiel), whose eyes are straining to see God (11:22); whose every fiber ascends to Him alone and won't descend until it finds Him.

20

Commending Heavenly Consolations

I'm your reward, more of a reward than you've ever hoped for.

(Genesis 15:1)

The Lord will rejoice when He hears the Soul speaking and won't hesitate to pick up the conversation.

"Yes, I'm your Beloved, the One and Only One." The words are from the Canticle of Canticles (VUL 5:10; NRSV Song of Solomon 5:10).

"I'm your reward, more of a reward than you've ever hoped for." These are the Lord's words to Abram in Genesis (15:1).

HERE, DEAR READER, are a few hints about your present earthly condition.

Be humble when things are going well.

When things aren't going all that well, be strong.

YES, SAID THE LORD, these were My earthly friends once. They did seem to enjoy My company. And once they've buried every human molestation of Soul and Body in the ground, they'll be able to establish permanent residence with Me in my rather spacious abode.

You, Lord, You entertain, You teach. You warm up Your audience when it's underheated, and You cool it off when it's overheated. You furl the sail, then unfurl it, then furl it again. You lead out, and You lead back. You shout *Advance!* You cry out *Retreat!* You do as You want with my Soul.

But I, Lord, I'm but a cracked and battered urn unable and indeed unworthy to hold the Spirit of God. Heavenly hugs and kisses await me, I know, and I seem to have had a foretaste of those sacred sweets, but I despair of ever being good enough to deserve the Full Banquet. And yet, even as I pray, even as I pore over my porous Soul, heavenly aromas wander in from the celestial patisserie.

Lord, You know how rare the thought of eternal things is, and how flimsy the thoughts are when they do come. Mouth waffles. Mind walks around in a daze. Conscience throws a fit. It's all my fault, and no other's!

But still exploring my Soul and the ways of my Soul, I keep going over and over all my secret assumptions about the Heavenly Life. What peace, what tranquility, what hope and exaltation, what eloquence and excellence — all in God our Savior!

Such delay as there may be from now till my death will be brief, and when it comes, it will be full of grace.

Whenever I'm thinking about the subject, God dims His illumination enough so that I can get a glimpse of what He means through my dark glass; that's to say, until I have some vague perception of the other side of the grave.

Yes, I had some real questions, some real complaints, and yet You, Lord, spoke to my Soul. I shushed all noise out of my life, and in the deathly silence that followed You spoke to me. Without words as intermediaries. And I heard You loud and clear. And yet the image that I have of myself is that of a derelict on the trash heap of creation. And yet You go out of Your way to console that derelict with strings and strings of wordless words, meanings without end.

HERE, LORD, is my prayerful reply.

Sad, the sinning Soul! Sad, the heaving conscience! Sad, the idle chatsworth! Sad, the one who has no luminous grace, no spiritual solace! Sad, the one who'd weep but just can't find the tears!

Happy, the Soul who keeps his eyes on Christ! He's the person who'll walk in peace and equity. No lout will break that trance. As for the external tumults, he'll distance himself from them, and soon he'll arrive at his new home.

TAKE A GOOD LOOK, dear Reader — that's how the Lord involves Himself in the lives of people He likes. If anyone comes to Him, he'll not leave empty-handed. The Lord's buttery is never bare; His treasury, never sparc.

My God, when You enter the house of the Soul who loves You, shouldn't You nurse that ailing Soul with something other than a pathetic corporeal image?

Then, dear Lord, You'll whisper in his ear Your most secret thoughts, all the good things You've done for him. Stuff about Eternal Rest and Communion of Saints. That way You'll make that ailing Soul stronger, more capable of hoping for the things it can't see, and spurning the things it can see.

Good Father, remember me, a poor pauper, a mealy mendicant from the bottommost cupboard of Your mercy! Do send from Heaven the True Bread, the True Word, high in grace, rich in consolation.

21

Traveling a Far Piece

I can't help but shout, "Lord, who else is there?"
(Psalm VUL 34:10; NRSV 35:10)

Yes, dear Reader, He's one of a kind and, like Him, well, there just isn't anybody else. No comparables. Nobody comes even close.

The Lord's my God.

He's my Beloved Friend, right out of the Canticle of Canticles (1:15), faithful *in excelsis,* the sort of person who never deserts the one who loves Him.

If I have a slip, get into trouble, find myself cornered, the Lord doesn't reprove me, tell me what a bum I am; rather He proves, purges, teaches me something. He may vanish from time to time, but He never really leaves; and in the meantime He shows just what kind of good friend He is.

WHAT AN ATTRACTIVE FELLOW HE IS, my Beloved Friend. Not as the eye of the Flesh sees Him, of course, but to the Mind's eye. To the Believing Soul, one who has a clean heart. One who's serious about conveying himself toward the invisibles and the spirituals.

DEAR READER, anyone who wants to become tight with the Lord, devotionally speaking, has to mortify himself, subdue every carnal affection, and keep his conscience pure, no matter how massive the attack.

If anything should tick you off, it should be someone tramping through the tulips with an eye toward scrounging some consolation from a creature!

You should know, dear Reader, the call to Consolation comes, not from the outside, but the inside. And as the Lord has already hinted, that call may come at any time.

How do I know this? Because I've caught Him red-handed, in the act, postponing me, putting me off as often as putting me on. Yes, and is it any wonder that I've had to conclude, it's really not so much what I want but what the Lord wants all the time! In a very real sense, I truly don't matter to Him.

About the best thing in the world that I can do is cultivate and indeed protect my relationship with Him for the lovely thing it is without trying to milk it for all it's worth. No cadging a souvenir during a visit. No making Avarice out of the Love.

THE LORD HAS LEFT ME many times, yes, but I myself have often traveled a far piece from Him! And Yes, I learned first-hand what He'd already taught me, that I may love other creatures and created things, but in the end they all wither and die.

IT ISN'T THAT creatures and created things are bad in and of themselves; they do praise the Lord in their own humble way. But in another, odd sort of way they may be said to achieve their Divine Goal if they set my own affections back on track to the Lord. After all, He's the One who made all creation, pulling rabbits out of hats, hats out of handkerchiefs, handkerchiefs out of nothings. And He's the one who grants me, of all people, to psalm His Holy Name like the Psalmist of Old (VUL 9:3; NRSV 9:2).

Yours is the Power, Lord! Yours the Wisdom! Yours, the Good-ness and the Piety! Yours, the Eternal Glory and Majesty! Yours, the Kingdom, the King for all ages! Yours, the Dominion, from generation to generation!.

"You manage all things well," as the Book of Wisdom put it (VUL 12:15; NRSV Wisdom of Solomon 12:15). You know every-thing in Your own mind. You hold everything in Your own hand. Nothing recoils from Your touch, nothing ruffles Your feathers. You praise as much as You appraise. The Defiant you turn into the Pli-ant. You know everything that's going on in the universe — even before it happens, You know how it'll turn out!

You're God of Heaven and Earth. You're Creator and Governor of the Visibles and Invisibles. You like timepieces that wind up and chimes that ring in the wind.

Preserve, save, keep as a whole, I beg You, Lord, Your servants scattered around the world, especially those recruited by You for Your Majesty's Secret Service. Make them sing Your praises and with one voice preach Your glory everywhere. Excite their hearts and stimulate them to emulate You. Grant to them all Your works so that they may turn them all to a good end.

O what a pious puss You put on for those who love You! How well You please those who enjoy Your company. Those who've ex-perienced Your smoothness in the classroom know from that how to think better and speak better.

The reason I say this is that Your sweetness makes all other sweeties seem like sour balls.

22

Sampling Divine Consolation

I'm the Consolation of all consolations!
(Exodus 3:14)

Dear Reader, the Holy Men of Old have spoken about the Lord; the Prophets themselves haven't held their tongues. Both believed in Him since the beginning of the world. They served Him, worshiped Him, kept His interest alive with gifts and offerings. They praised His Holy Name, blessed His Holy Name, because they knew that He was the Creator of all things. They recognized Him in their visions. They stood sentinel over the Law as it was contained in the Commandments. They weren't taken in by silly images of false gods; rather they adored the living God who created all images. They lifted up their voices in praise because He came down from on high and filled their ears with the sound of silver tinkling. This is what He said.

I am who I am — an echo from the Exodist (3:14).

Before Me there was nothing like Me — an echo from Isaiah (43:10–11).

THE HOLY PEOPLE of Old heard these things and understood them, raised their faithful eyes from afar, believing the Lord would make them safe forever. Yes, He'll come when He'll come. And that's no lie.

This sort of foreknowledge warmed their souls and changed their attitude toward the Divine to one of awe and respect. And this was their breathless prayer.

You are who You are — an echo from the prophet Isaiah (43:10–11).

You are our Lord God — there is no other.

You captured us, and You'll save us. You can't say no to Yourself, deny Yourself as though You weren't true — an echo of Paul's Second to Timothy (2:13). As we've heard, so we've seen. As we believe, so we speak. As we testify, so we testify to its truthfulness.

YES, GOD SPOKE in Genesis (1:3), stuff was created, and the following warning was recorded.

My counsel will stand, and Your counsel, coming as it does from the Son of Man, will die — an echo from Isaiah (46:10).

Woe to you who think that counsel less than useful, worth only a good laugh behind God's back! Sounds like Micah (2:1).

Woe to those of you who make up some wisdom from your heart's own experience instead of drawing on the experience of the Scriptures!

Hear the word of the Lord, you who quest for the Lord — sounds like Osee (4:1). Know that it's his judgment that will judge the inhabitants of the earth.

Turning away from the Lord — that's not a good thing. Take a stand today and review your point of view.

YES, DEAR READER, reverse your course and come back to where you belong. The Lord'll willingly review your case. Why? Because, as He's proven so many times, He's forgiving to a fault.

He knows what anger is. If thunder and lightning have any meaning at all, He has moments of anger Himself, but it's not the sort of anger human beings flare up into. And unlike Humankind, He's quick to forgive sins. Moreover, He has this lovely habit of folding Prior Grace into Posterior Grace.

What's the moral for us, dear Reader?

With a full conversion in our hearts, forgive those who also serve with faithful mind.

TRANSLATION, LITERAL OR PARAPHRASAL

How is it that *Consolations,* written in fifteenth-century Latin, reads like twenty-first century English? That's to say, isn't this translation too free, too racy, too irreverent, to be right? Can it possibly represent what must surely have been a fairly dull Latin text?

The answer to the second question is no; to the third, yes. Perhaps some definitions will help.

There are least two theories of translation.

Literal translation, the method favored by academics, strives to be faithful to the Latin text; that's to say, it translates every Latin word into an English word. Denotations only; no connotations. If the Latin sentence has one hundred words, then the English sentence must have at least a hundred words. And so on. Fidelity is the cardinal virtue of literal translation, but sometimes it can turn into a cardinal sin; that's to say, no matter how the literal translator lumbers on, the translated passage may turn out to be more obscure than the Latin.

Paraphrasal translation, on the other hand, has a fidelity of its own, but to the meaning of a Latin passage, not to its wording. Denotations, yes, but connotations too. If the Latin sentence has a hundred words, then the paraphrase will also have a hundred words, but more likely in ten sentences of ten words each; more likely still, it may have ten sentences but perhaps with a word total of two hundred, perhaps even three hundred words.

An illustration, if I may, taken from Kempis's *Imitation of Christ* (Book 2, Chapter 11).

LATIN   *Multi miracula eius venerantur;*
               pauci ignominiam crucis sequuntur.

LITERAL   Many venerate His miracles; few
               follow the ignominy of His cross.

PARAPHRASAL   Many are wowed by His miracles;
               few are wooed by His cross.

The difference between literal and paraphrasal is remarkable, and indeed desirable.

Some observations on translations.

1. All translations from Latin into English, including this one, good as they may seem, are bound to fail. That's to say, if a translation catches as much as 25 percent of the Latin original, then it's done well.

2. Caution! Paraphrasal translation may convey the meaning of a text well, but it should never be used in school exercises. Scholarship requires that a paraphrasal translation, if used at all, should be used only in conjunction with a literal translation and the Latin original.

3. Paraphrasal translation requires, at the very least, partial mastery of Latin but complete mastery of

English. With literal translation by academics, it's the other way round. They're mightily equipped in the foreign but woefully equipped in the mother tongue.

4. To the principles of translation, literal or paraphrasal, must be added the principles of modern communication — a comparatively new, still a rough and roguish, science. It has the audacity to say that when one wants to communicate, one must do so to a sizable segment of the literate population, not to a pitiful few — or die! Which is another way of saying, it must pay its own way. Alas, literal translators, who are mostly academics, work under no such pressure and, hence, it's no wonder that their translations have wobbly legs.

5. A corollary to the preceding. Paraphrasal translations must not only enlighten but also entertain.

6. In the morning one may do a paraphrasal translation of a given passage. In the afternoon, the translator, forgetting that he'd already translated the same passage, may translate it again. Odd thing, though; it will almost certainly turn out differently, even unrecognizably, though just as reliably and remarkably. How can that happen? it seems to me I hear you ask. The translator used whatever tropes and figures came to mind at the moment of translation.

Perhaps it's better, after all these things about translation theory have been said, to learn to read and enjoy the original language. —W.G.

23

Walking into an Ambush

*The one thing you don't want to do
is walk right into an ambush.*

(Matthew 14:38)

Hear those voices? The Saints! Like magpies chattering in the cloister, melodies thrumming in the banquet hall, aromas rising from the thurible. That's what God's Word is like in a pure heart; that's what the Saints sound like. They're the living memory of the Lord's past extravagance and eloquence.

A note in passing, dear Reader. My conversation with you today through the written word may appear rather pedestrian. That's to say, it doesn't have the legs to ascend to a higher plane. But if fire should come down from above, if lightning hits my eloquence, then it'll consume me before it consumes you. Up and down, up and down—just give me a touch, and I'll fly right off.

If and when that happens, there'll be no past, and the future won't count. All bad things will slip into oblivion. Old baggage will be lost, only to be replaced by new. Holy desires will gush and, from every side, they'll surge together wherever the Sweet Spirit flows. No fear no more. Only Love will flow to overflow. Bickering and brawling'll stagger to a halt.

How will all this come about? It'll come from the right hand of God. So what I've said, well, it's praise, not mine, but His.

So WHAT ARE the Saints saying?

There's consolation for the Mourner, some bread for the Beggar, a draft for the Parched!

A hand is given to the Ill, a crutch to the Lame!

The Helpless recover, the Restless find rest!

For the Desperate new light has arisen; for the Shouter comes a response at last!

For the Fog-bound a light begins to glow; for the Lost the dark becomes high noon!

For the Doubter Truth taps him on the shoulder!

For the Undecided authority will make up his mind!

For the Persistent Inquirer Mother Charity appears in the middle of the road!

For the one desiring to speak to the Beloved He'll joyfully oblige!

So, how'll you respond? asked the Lord of the Soul. What'll you suffer and do for me?

So YOU SEE, dear Reader, with saintly voices like that ringing in my ears, it's no wonder that my Soul flies off on a tear. Immediately I forget how dirty, how unclean I felt back on earth. My one desire was to live with my Beloved Friend but, well, He didn't want to come right out and say no. He did manage, though, to give me the bad news, but with soft and gentle voice. It just wasn't the thing to do, He said; at least not now.

WHAT THE LORD SAID went something like this.

Your desire's good, and your prayer is always pleasing. But you might want to do one thing. Go and tell the people you know and come in contact with how much I did for You. Particularly tell them this.

"Each and every one of you, prep your hearts and dump your sins. Be on the lookout, the Devil's traps and tropes are all around you."

"Watch and pray," said Jesus to the lads in the Garden of Gethsemane (Matthew 14:38); "the one thing you don't want to do is walk right into an ambush."

Yes, dear Soul, I'm coming and, yes, the time draws near. When you do see Me coming down the road, do sound the alarum, and don't say I didn't warn you!

24

Looking for
a Better Deal

"Say to my Soul," said the Psalmist to the Lord,
" 'Yes, I'm your Salvation.' "

(Psalm VUL 34:3; NRSV 35:3)

How marvelous, Soul of my Soul! How absolutely marvelous!
Bulbs today, lilies tomorrow! What wonders lie within!

One such wonder catches my fancy. If I could have it, I'd
be content. And have it I must. Now. No shilly, no shally! No
substitutes, no stand-ins. I've tried them all.

So what is this one thing?

Well, I don't know exactly. But I don't think I can find it in
the marketplaces of the world. Maybe it's not a created thing
at all. It's definitely a good. Perhaps the Good, perhaps the
only Good, perhaps the only God who, as the Psalmist would
put it, "clings to me and I to Him" (VUL 72:28; NRSV 73:28).

"So," says my Soul to the Lord, "that's why I'm speaking to
You in this way, making a fuss about it, shouting it out loud.
Tell me the words I want to hear — *I'm your Salvation!*"

"Yes, dear Soul," said the Lord. "Indeed I'm your Salvation.
And why wouldn't I be? You cling to Me, so why wouldn't I
cling to you?"

"Yes, Lord, but sometimes I lose my grasp and, to prevent my complete and utter fall, I have to grasp another."

"But why would you do that? I'm the strongest vine of them all. Is it that you want to test every other vine before you finally rely on Me?"

"Something like that."

"You're shopping around, aren't you?" asked the Lord. "Looking for a better deal? Well, shop the souks of the world if you want. Others do it. First one looks for a villa; second starts a business; third opens a bank; fourth has to entertain his business associates; fifth sets out to see the world; sixth hangs out his shingle as a wisdom figure; seventh swans around like a duke or a prince. Excuses, excuses, excuses! They remind me of the people who said they couldn't come to the wedding" (Luke 14:18–19).

Few seek the One purely and simply for Himself and for no other reason. Most, I must admit, cloud their own minds into thinking that they need at least one thing from the secular world in order to survive. That's not to say they don't find Peace or Grace; they do, but, as Paul noted in his to the Philippians, it's a fragile Peace they find, a fractured, fragmented Grace (2:21).

There are other people, even Christ's own, who feel quite at home with created things, but don't really consider them indispensable possessions. Perhaps they have some wisdom they'd like to share with us on this prickly subject.

Well, I'll ask this question of you, Soul of my Soul — *Do you consider any of your possessions indispensable?* — and I'm also going to answer it myself. *Certainly not!* I detest all these things. The One-and-Only is my good, my sort of good. He's the One I love, and the One I need, and the One I treasure more than all the other goods above and below.

If you should stumble upon that Good one day, I urge you, persuade you, to guard it and hold on to it for all you're worth!

25

Letting Go

For God's sake, leave father and mother behind.
(Genesis 2:24; Matthew 19:5; Mark 10:7; Ephesians 5:31)

Letting go of creatures and created things won't break your back, dear Soul, or even your heart. In fact, you may find it well worth your while. In truth, to give all and suffer all is just about everything you should want to do in life.

So do continue your quest for the perfect created thing. But as long as you're wearing that body bag, you're bound to come up empty-handed.

"How WILL I KNOW when the search is over?"

"When the party begins," replied the Lord.

"But how will I know when the party begins?"

"I had these lovely invitations engraved," replied the Lord.

"But, lovely as it is, it doesn't give the place or the time."

"Well, it won't take place in this world, I can assure you of that," replied the Lord. "As for the time, I haven't set it yet."

"What about created things?"

"You'll have to turn them in at the gate," replied the Lord.

"Then I may have to crash the gate."

"Security guards!" warned the Lord.

"You've thought of everything."

"Remember," said the Lord, "only when you've emptied your hands and enter empty-handed will you find your hands full, full of the hands of the Singular Solitary, the One and Only."

DIVINE PIETY — that's what I'm urging on you, dear Reader. It's hard to describe. Perhaps I should point out some of its signs.

For every Bride there will be a Groom; for every Child, a Father.

The Sick will have a Doctor. The Healthy, solid food. The Ignorant, Teachers. The Obedient, Eternal Life.

Beginners will need special help

Penitents will have hope; the Just console best. The Humble will be raised up; the Proud, laid low.

Shadows now, chandeliers then.

For those sad and depressed about the past, there's always Beaujolais nouveau!

He stands with us when we're fighting. He walks with us when we're out for a stroll. He runs with the fervent; He flies with the contemplatives; He leads a merry chase.

He's present when we're praying. He talks when we read. He settles in when we meditate.

In all of these the One-and-the-Same God is at work and, upon investigation, we can find His personal touch everywhere.

Of course, He could beat up on us, but He doesn't; and He doesn't run down a checklist of our maladies and badger us to do better.

His humongous imprint is felt on all things, though. No pussyfooting about for Him. And yet, in the end, no one knows why He really favors this rather than that.

GENDER, HISTORICAL OR CONTEMPORARY

The continuing feminist movement to introduce gender equality into historical documents is a noble, and indeed a necessary, one.

A good example of what's wrong about historical gender today may be found in this very book, *Consolations for My Soul*. When one reads it for the first time — and you, dear Reader, have to be reading it for the first time, for in its five-hundred-year history it has appeared in English translation perhaps once, perhaps twice — one can't help but feel it was written by and for the Men's Club.

Kempis himself, a collective noun for himself and two or three others, all founders of the Brothers of the Common life, was part of the problem; he was also an Augustinian monk and priest. His reading audience came from all these groups during his lifetime and for similar groups since his death in 1471. Perhaps it's not surprising that all his references and referent points are masculine in form and reality.

Another part of the gender problem is Latin, the language Kempis and other early and medieval spiritual writers wrote in. It has the traditional three genders: masculine, feminine, and neuter. The first, third, and fifth declensions are dedicated to feminine nouns; the second and fourth, to masculine nouns; the third, to all three.

Odd thing, though. In the first declension there's a group of nouns that are feminine in form but masculine in gender. *Nauta* (sailor) and *agricola* (farmer) are the usual suspects trotted out by grammarians. But in the long and meandering history of the Latin language there are perhaps hundreds, perhaps thousands, of nouns in this mischievous class.

Personal pronouns are equally rascally when it comes to genderizing ancient languages. They may be either masculine or feminine as the occasion demands. But the masculine in a good number of cases also includes the feminine, especially in the plural.

Plural nouns of any declension may often be translated as male or female. *Viri* may come through as "men" but also as "men and women." And the opposite seems to be true, although the classical grammarians, dead as dodoes for at least a century now, have yet to discover it. *Mulieres* may be rendered not only as "women" but also as "men and women, but especially women."

For better or worse, masculine and feminine genders in the ancient languages have inevitably been intertwined with each other, and perhaps that's as it should be. Not that there's anything wrong with that.

Historical confusion of genders appears mightily in drama. Playwrights wrote luscious female parts, even though they had to be played by male actors. In ancient Greece men in buskins played such grisly dramatic heavyweights as Clytemnestra, Electra, and Medea; and in Shakespearean drama callow male youths played such dreamy wisps as Juliet, Rosalind, Desdemona, and such deadly wasps as Beatrice, Lady Macbeth, Cleopatra.

Yes, *Consolations* partakes of all the historical gender confusions of its own time but also in its own holy and hoary tradition of spiritual writing down to the present day. But perhaps, just perhaps, *Consolations* is also an instance of what's right. Kempis created two male characters, the Lord and the Soul. Their dialogue ranges from trash talk to talk that's truly divine — all the sort of talk one would expect to find in a strong male friendship and, in this case, a strong male spiritual friendship. Far from finding all this masculinity offending, this paraphrasal translator has played it for all its worth, with some surprisingly vivid and memorable results.

Parenthetically, as if to make matters worse, in what can only be construed as moments of madness, Kempis hotted up his already red-hot male friendship with some white-hot heterosexual quotations from the Canticle of Canticles (Song of Solomon). What's a translator to do? I choose to delve further into the deep heaven of a text and, far from ending up in a cul-de-sac, I may just emerge into the bright sunlight of universality.

Two final points.

First, I consider Latin a living language, not just a secular language that languished in the first century of the Christian era and has never recovered. Such literature as it produced through the so-called golden and silver periods was nice, but just a piddle when compared with what Latin has produced in the last two thousand years. Even the humble *nauta,* which used to denote only "male sailor," now sports "female sailor," even "First Lady of the Admiralty" *(nauta primissima).*

Second, the Sistern of the Common Life was a para-group of the Brethren; it had three times as many communities as the men. To these holy women the ragged materials that make up *Consolations* were used to give spiritual conferences. That's why there's every chance that a modern female translator, using techniques of para-phrasal rather than literal translation, would capture not only the meaning of the text of *Consolations* but also the texture of the meaning; at least as the Sistern them-selves would've understood — and women today would understand — it. I look forward to that day, hopefully in the nearest future, with greatest enthusiasm.

All of which is to say, historically wronged as femi-nists surely have been, the remedy has to be more than feminizing the godhead and putting pinnies on all the personal pronouns; it's in the vulgar yet learned para-phrasing of the offending classics. That's to say, it lies in feminizing the details — as I have masculinized the details — of *Consolations.* — W.G.

26

Trailing the Lord

Why do you hide Your face from me, Lord?

(Job 13:24)

Some things have to be said.

Humankind isn't at its best when it grills the Omnipotent with trick questions.

Every invention of the sons of Adam, created things all, all are empty and vain.

God's just — I think we can agree on this — so how can one argue with Him about Justice?

WHY THE FUSS? Why do you ask? Why do you seek the explanation of everything, the *Totum Bonum*, in infinite detail? It's like walking on a foggy night. Perhaps a warm glow ahead, perhaps a lamppost, perhaps even a figure leaning against the lamppost. It's all so mysterious.

My point here is that we can't conclude much about God's principle or indeed His end. As Paul wrote to the Romans, there's no need to bump one's head against the sky when trying to explain Heaven (11:20). Jesus Son of Sirach (3:22) and the Proverbialist (25:27) said much the same thing.

Perhaps it's better to expend our energy meditating on Jesus and the humility He surrounded Himself with while on earth, from His birth to His death. Of course, one has to admit that in creating the universe, with all of its hangings and fittings, He had a decorous touch.

O JESUS, *You Who Must Be Embraced, I'd freely follow You around the world, though You'd rather I followed You into Heaven. If I remember Your words in Matthew aright, that's where Your treasure is, and that's where my heart should be (6:21).*

Yes, You are my treasure, Lord, right at the right hand of the Father. Incarnated for my benefit, revelated in my behalf. You left Yourself as an example on earth; in Heaven You Yourself are the reward.

Therefore, my eyes will be on You, my steps will traipse after You. To You my heart echoes the Psalmist. "My face searches for You; for Your face, O Lord, I need to see" (VUL 26:8; NRSV 27:8). How long, O Lord, before I see the vision of Your face?

WHY DO YOU HIDE *Your face from me, Lord? Job asked the same question (13:24). Is it that You think I'm Your enemy?*

You know my Soul hithers and thithers, sometimes even slithers; that's to say, my affections are pulled from pillar to post. Hopefully, they'll be joined to You in Heaven as friend to Friend.

Odd thing about Love. It just doesn't know how or when to quit or when to sit down in a corner and think of nothing but God. It just wants to hunt its lover down, send urgent messages, repeat petitionary prayers, mumble over rosary beads — that's to say, collect everything that belongs to the Beloved, every eyelash, every toenail, every piece of evidence.

Therefore, the obvious, Lord. You have to make Yourself a big enough attraction so that I'll follow you, run after You, not deny You in public. For unless You do stuff like this, no one'll volunteer to be the dragged.

Look back and see whether I'm following You, Lord. If I'm nowhere in sight, wait for me to catch up, then give me Your hand. But if You were to give me Your hand, I'd skip in front of You. The faster I'd run, the faster You'd have to run to keep up.

When I falter, then egg me on."When I'll be exalted from the earth," I remember Your saying in John, "I'll draw You after me" (12:32).

So, Soul of mine, what gets in your way that you want to leave all behind to join Jesus, but just can't bring yourself to do it? Why are you so loath to leave behind the vanishables and perishables?

Window-shop till you drop — what comfort does that give you?

Look, when you pass through the visibles, trying to find some content in them, you kill the better things in life. From the *Summum Bonum* you divide yourself when you do this and turn yourself away from true and blessed and eternal life. Wretched and unhappy you'll remain, full of high anxiety.

Whichever way you turn, you'll find dolors and doldrums galore. Turn yourself around and head back to the Creator. He's your Peace and Quiet.

So don't delay, stop your false starts, get a move on, don't make so much as a convenience stop, and by all means don't stop to admire the flowers. And don't for a moment stop to venerate that fuzzy image of yourself in the mirror; just wait for the perfect mirror image that won't die.

When you leaf through all the visibles, not to enjoy them in and of themselves, but to use them to construct a ladder whose rungs will support your climb to Heaven, then two things'll happen. First, you'll be liberated from all the sludge of the Present Age. Second, you'll be wooed with the fudge of the Next Age. All this through God, the Blessed One down the Ages.

27

Clinging for Dear Life

Lord, my Soul's clinging to You for dear life!
(Psalm VUL 62:9; NRSV 63:9)

Dear Lord, Consoler of the Doleful Soul, can we talk? I need to talk. Yes, it'll be boring, but to You, not to me. I have this secret fear....

If I die in the next hour, who'll know? Who'll tell You? But why would You want to know?

You're the Above-All, the One-and-Only. I'm the Beneath-It-All, the One-among-Many.

You're in Heaven; I'm in the world.

You, the Alone, the Most High; I, just a face in the crowd, and a dirty face at that.

Who has measured the distance between Heaven and Earth? It's too great, and You're too far away from me.

Who'll bring us together? You're going to have to do it, or no one's going to do it. But if You want to do it, then make it happen quickly.

Why?

Because I have this habit of tripping up, falling all over myself. But without You I can't stand, let alone make progress. Yes, my Soul hangs by a spiritual thread and by an infusion of Salutary Grace.

Just say the word, and my Soul will be elevated, escalated from Earth. Just turn Your head the other way, and my Soul won't seem so discombobulated.

Because of Your paternal custom and usage, I know You'll take my hand and lead me along the path through the garden to Your heavenly home.

CHILDREN OF THE EARTH, give me your ears, as the Psalmist cried out! It's both possible, and indeed quite easy, to find oneself, whether rich or poor, in the presence of God (VUL 48:2–3; NRSV 49:1–2). Owing, as I do, something to just about everybody in this world and the next, I'm the pauper in that story. Owing nothing to anybody — that's the Rich Man, God.

If you don't have much experience in this sort of thing, dear Reader, I have reliable proof that a soul, any soul, can be united with God through grace. "My Beloved told me — I found him grazing with his flock." This is the testimony of the Bride and the Groom in Canticle of Canticles (VUL 2:11; NRSV Song of Solomon 2:11). Theirs is the witness of the Sacred Law in the Old Testament.

Another valid witness appears in the New Testament, Gospel of John. "Father, You and I, we two are one, so why shouldn't we be one with everyone else?" (17:11).

In these two Testaments it can quickly and easily be discovered how the Soul may join the inner circle with God. It's Heavenly Grace that does the trick.

Such a phenomenon may be rare, but it's the sweeter for its rarity. In other words, it's difficult but not out of the question.

But just how does God pull it off? Well, who'd be so churlish as to try to separate someone from God or raise a fuss about God's getting His priorities right?

If you're stunned by the outrageousness of this on-again off-again friendship, then you're in the enviable position of being able to study it firsthand, and thereby admire the excellence of His goodness.

After all, the Lord has the license to do whatever He wants. Of course, He's also licensed to do the big miracles (Psalm VUL 135:4; NRSV 136:2).

By the way, dear Reader, if you want to know who authorized this friendship, you'll find out that He was the One. In return, the Soul turned his back on worldly things but somehow still finds ways to mess up the friendship.

O, dear Soul, to be with Christ and have Christ take you under his wings!

But woe to you also, dear Soul, when He does His famous vanishing act. You'll fall into bad humor and nothing'll seem to go your way. Grace will stop flowing, Scripture will lose its meaning, prayer will grow tedious, meditation will grind to a halt, the clouds of the heart will portend a deluge, toxic thoughts will prevail. Simultaneously, or so it seems, your happy world will collapse around you!

28

Complaining Loudly to an Absent Friend

The bitterness in my Soul cries to High Heaven!
(Job 7:11)

Lord God, why do You behave this way? Is this some sort of game You're playing? Are you really the pious Jesus or just another goofy pretender?

YES, I HAVE ISSUES, and the main one I want to talk about right here and now is this. You spend more time talking with others than You do with me. Of course, I know by now that You're a control freak, operating on an unforgiving schedule I know not of, but I'd just like to see greater latitude in the colloquies between You and me.

Routinely, in Your official capacity, You see sinners, souls in distress. I know because I can hear You and Your patients talking and carrying on in Your office. But here I am, out in the anteroom, unable to obtain an appointment, forced to twiddle my thumbs even as I'm dying the death!

Is it any wonder that I flee Your office before it's my turn? Is it any wonder that I wake up in the middle of the night screaming Your name? Can't You recognize a cry for help when You hear one?

Yes, Lord, You beat up on sinners; we've all felt Your lash. But perhaps we should be the ones beating up on You.

You're big on the Real Presence, I must say, but that's not our problem. Our problem is the Real Absence. You're never there when we need You. While You're chatting up another patient or just going out to lunch, the truly Desolate Soul sits in Your anteroom reading old magazines.

Yes, I know I must pray whether You're present or absent. But when You're absent, the Enemy is always present working all sorts of mischief.

When You finally do show up, dear Lord, You come as the Prodigal expecting a great welcome. Well, You have it upside down. We the sinners are the prodigals, and You're supposed to welcome us back, not the other way round. Trouble with all the joy behind the festivities when You return is that we poor blokes think You'll never leave again.

You're here, dear Lord, but Your mind is elsewhere. You have that guilty, naughty-boy look. You're already planning Your next move. Then, for no apparent reason, You withdraw. The Soul doesn't make anything of it at first but, on the hundredth such occasion, he finally catches on.

You leave Your message, and then You're off. Is that any way to treat a beloved friend like me? Do You really think the neighbors will construe Your staying any longer as a scandal? Do You have any documentation on this phenomenon? If so, I demand to see it.

When someone puts it to You like this, Lord, I notice Your demeanor changes, but there's no way to read Your mind. You play it close to the vest, which You don't really need to do. You win. You always win. Who's complaining? Well, we the sinners are!

Up to this point, Lord, mine would be only a minor complaint if You had the good grace to bring it up openly. Something like, "I come and I go." "It's the sort of thing I do." If You just said something like this, nobody'd think You should do more.

No, You don't say that. Surely You know how to speak in proverbs, and yet You've offered no proverb, no excuse, no rationale, no alibi. The only thing You come up with is Your Word. In the past Your Word has had currency. Now I'm beginning to wonder.

My complaint may be a loud one, Lord, but in a good sense. It isn't that I don't want to hear Your side. I'll keep an open soul. Do respond whenever you think it the right moment.

But as one of Your Devouts I reserve the right, when You finally do give Your explanation, to lower the boom, or at the very least to put a question or two whenever I feel You've been less than forthcoming.

Again, as I say, take all the time You need. I'll give You the benefit of every doubt. And, of course, complete confidentiality. For my ears only. I see no reason why Your reputation should have to suffer. But if Your confession should make You sad, I may have to console You, the lesser offering Kleenex to the greater. What larks!

So Lord, I end where I began.

When the flow of Your grace trickles to a drop, I get antsy and anxious and cry out.

You used to suffer fools gladly, but somewhere along the line You left this fool behind.

Will we ever talk again?

Will we ever have a nice sit-down?

Will we ever have another one-on-one?

REAL PRESENCE
AND ABSENCE

Now you see Him — now you don't!

Here one moment — gone the next!

First date, kiss, fervor — end of affair, romance, friendship!

To hear mystics talk about their miserable lives — and Kempis was a mystic — the mystical life hasn't been all it's cracked up to be.

About the best the scholars of mysticism can conclude is, it's apophatic one moment, cataphatic the next; that's to say, dark night of the soul one moment, high noon the next.

So what's really going on here? Is it illusionism, prestidigitation, legerdemain on the part of the Divine?

One scholar, Bernard McGinn, Divinity School, University of Chicago, put it this way.

"The paradoxical necessity of both presence and absence is one of the most important of all the verbal strategies by means of which mystical transformation has been symbolized. The relationship has been portrayed in many forms.

"Sometimes, among the more positive, or cataphatic, mystics, it is primarily a successive experience, as in the coming and going of the Divine Lover presented in the Song of Songs [Canticle of Canticles] and studied by the great mystical commentators on the Song, such as Origen and Bernard of Clairvaux.

"At other times, among the negative or apophatic mystics, presence and absence are more paradoxically and dialectically simultaneous."

—Bernard McGinn, *The Foundations of Mysticism,* vol. 1 of *The Presence of God: A History of Western Christian Mysticism* (New York: Crossroad, 1991), p. xviii.

All of which is, perhaps, another way of saying, the Divine may be both absent and present at one and the same time in one and the same place. The way we know that He's present, even though He seems absent, is that He actually can't leave the premises even if He wants to. How's that possible?

Well, if one considers the metaphysics of it (divine properties like omnipresence, immensity, uncontainability) as well as the physics of it (physical dimensions like a small room with a small door), then it's no wonder He can't leave. He can't fit through the doorway!

Ah, well, where's the Great Houdini when you need him? I'm being whimsical, of course, but I fare no worse than the Great McGinn when trying to describe the indescribable.

All that being said, no better expression of the bipolarity of the soul in the history of mysticism can be found than in the preceding chapter, "Complaining Loudly to an Absent Friend."

End of comments on the problems that the absence of one party can cause in another.

Alas, the presence of both parties has problems of its own; chief among them is gender.

Kempis has created two characters, male and male, the Lord and the Soul; the former, alternately the First and Second Persons of the Trinity; the latter, the soul of Kempis himself.

Trouble is when Kempis quotes or alludes to the Canticle (Song), a cataphatic indicator if there ever was one, the implication is that the Lord is the Groom and the Soul is the Bride. That, it seems to me, casts an unusual light on whether the spiritual friendship between Lord and Soul is heterosexual or homosexual.

Isn't this the question one shouldn't, needn't, really ask? But what's a paraphrasal translator to do? After all, it's not so much in the details as in the words the translator chooses to use. I chose to emphasize the strong male friendship between Lord and Soul. No Baryshnikov bursting from the Bridal Suite in this translation of *Consolations!*

Clearly, these are considerations that never occurred to Kempis or other medieval writers. It's just that modern paraphrasal translators must meet such consideration head on, make decisions, and reveal them to the Reader. Which is another way of saying, it's in the words. What better place to be! —W.G.

29

Pining for the Beloved

Bored to tears, my Soul nodded off.
(Psalm VUL 118:28; NRSV 119:28)

I had this dream, said the Soul. I found myself thrust into the Canticle of Canticles (NRSV Song of Solomon) where I met a Stranger in a cloak. He asked me my story, and this was what I said.

"I've lost my Beloved Friend, and I've been looking for Him everywhere. I kept calling His name, but heard nothing in return until, bushed, exhausted, as the Psalmist would say, my Soul nodded off" (VUL 118:28; NRSV 119:28).

"Did you lose your friend, dear Soul, or did He lose you?"

"He lost me, and I don't know why," said the Soul. "As far as I'm concerned, I did everything He asked of me. I gave up everything for Him."

"I can see how that took you by surprise," said the Stranger, drying the Soul's eyes with his handkerchief.

"I can remember the first time I met Him," said the Soul, his eyes still damp. "He came skipping on the mountains, right up to the gates of my house."

"Is that how you remember it, or did it happen just that way?"

"Well, of course, not exactly like that,"said the Soul, "but how did you know?"

"I think I may have heard this story before, but do continue. It never ceases to please."

"Well, He turned my life around. Immediately I knew I had to slam shut the gates of the flesh after Him, and I gave my new friend a hearty welcome. We sat together for a long while, I remember, shielded from the wind and the rain by an umbrella."

"What did He mean to you?" asked the Stranger.

"Well, I just felt good in His presence," said the Soul. "He made me happy. He made my heart skip faster. I can only imagine that He had the same reaction. We'd say a few things, and then we wouldn't say a thing. We'd just sit there, enjoying each other's company."

"Was this really your first meeting, or had your paths crossed before?" asked the Stranger.

"We knew each other by sight," remembered the Soul, "but this was the first time we'd sat down together. In that sense He was, of course, a new friend."

"What did you talk about?" asked the Stranger.

"Well, I think that's rather private, just between the two of us. But I do think I can say, without violating His privacy, that He teased me. Nothing insipid, mind you, but all rather funny. We laughed a lot. Not a dull moment. With Him gone now, my poor heart is surely going to burst!"

"Why's that?" asked the Stranger.

"I have no other distraction now, except perhaps deploring His absence. He was everything I ever hoped for in a friend. And He was so inventive when it came to joy — He never repeated himself once."

"Well, that's rather rare in a friend," said the Stranger in passing comment.

"My wish became his wish. And whatever he cooked up became my delight. I just kept telling more and more about myself, and He didn't seem to lose interest. We became one in heart and mind, and a great tranquillity descended upon us."

"Such a story!" said the Stranger. "At least your version of it. Do tell it again. More slowly this time so we can enjoy each and every detail!"

As you may have guessed by now, dear Reader, and as I guessed sometime later, the Stranger I was talking to so pleasantly was the Lord Himself dressed in a velvet cloak.

30

Being Hung Out to Dry

Blessed is the God who hasn't hauled off
and moved His mercy elsewhere.

(Psalm VUL 65:20; NRSV 66:20)

Dear Keeper of my Soul, it's happened again. My Beloved Friend has given me the pious once-over and found me wanting; that's to say, not ready for His company full time. So what am I supposed to do? Twiddle my thumbs? Consult my books? Climb the highest hill and halloo Him until He halloos back?

There's one thing you shouldn't do, dear Soul. Don't stop your pious chitchat. From this sort of one-way conversation He can tell whether your pain is real or made up. The reason I say this is that He sees you happy sometimes; sad sometimes; sometimes puddle-jumping, other times just standing right smack in the middle of the muck.

The cause of these mood swings I judge to be precisely this, the to-ing and fro-ing, hithering and thithering of your Beloved Friend. He's hung you out to dry many times over. That's what I think.

And another thought. You have issues you'd like to talk over with Him, but if He's not there, they just keep churning inside of you. Of course, all this would go away if He'd just show up more often and stay longer.

The nice thing about being with Him, said the Soul to his Keeper, is that He talks, but He lets me do more than my share, and then my time is up before I've really had a chance to make my point.

Yes, said the friendly Keeper, but one sure way to get Him back is to gather a few friends together and start talking about Him. That should do it quite nicely. I wouldn't ordinarily propose this to you since one-on-one time is what you want. But it does seems to be His custom, to show up when a few of His very best friends gather round.

Yes, said the Soul to his Friend, love is what brings our little group together. We're happy together, sad together, and mutual love is really the point of it all.

Which is another way of saying, said the Keeper, Woe to the loner, the solitary cyclist, falling into a ditch; that's to say, subject to depression and temptation! He has no one to help him out or cheer him up. But if there are two brothers, then one can keep the fire kindled in the other. Or so Eccesiastes once proposed (4:10–11).

These ups and downs don't seem to have a definite cause, but they can be ticked off by adversity and or a crying fit. That's where two Devouts are better than one. They can help each other keep an even keel, keep the rumpus down to a roar, that sort of thing. Could this sad condition be improved if two brothers lived in the same house? The Psalmist thought so (VUL 132:1; NRSV 133:1).

Thank you for your kind thoughts, said the Soul to his Friend. I feel I can talk with you. I don't have to fear what you say. And I don't have to worry about making stupid remarks.

SPENDING TIME WITH THE LORD — what was it like? asked the Keeper.

Well, said the Soul, thank God He's attracted to wretches like me! Even when I'm not myself, He allows me to enjoy the warmth of our presence together. He brought about my being reborn through the Grace of Baptism, and He's clothed me with the glory of His merits.

Up to the time we first met, I'd done nothing but deform myself, befoul myself, beset myself with my sins. I'd forgotten what it was to have a friend. But the Lord had a glad eye when we first met up, and He didn't say a word about how badly I needed a bath. Nonetheless, discreetly, He saw to it that I had one.

Yes, that first day began with Him a long way off, too far for me to see, but I heard Him hallooing me through His grace, promising that He was coming to save me from the sort of death this world brings. When He finally arrived, He provided me with a cottage, where I could pause awhile to catch my breath; that's to say, to stay until I'd spent my last breath.

OF COURSE, it wasn't really a getaway, said the Soul, nor was it really a breather from the harum-scarum of everyday life. There weren't anything like days or nights. But it did provide a pleasant pause, and I was indeed able to shed a few everyday cares. Fewer distractions, finer conversations. Not that many frills, though, and even the temptations were primal, basic, meat-and-potato ones. He assured me I could handle them, and He even gave me a few tips on just how to do it. And every now and then it rained, the Lord's way of seeing to it that I received enough Grace and Consolation from above.

31

Remembering a Friend

We haven't forgotten Your faith and love, Lord.
(1 Thessalonians 1:3)

Some of the things the Lord said to me during happier times.

"If you want Me, you'll hear Me."

"If you want to look around, drink in the surroundings — don't let the opportunity pass."

"If you do what I say, you'll be My friend."

"If you choose Me instead of anyone else, you'll be My very special friend."

"Whatever you ask will come to you from the Father."

"If you should decide to kiss Me off, you'll find yourself out on your ear."

"If you come to think that one Best Friend isn't enough and start looking for another, that poor sap won't be your friend long; I'll turn him against you. Why? Because I'm your Salvation, and nobody else!"

So much for the quotable quotes, dear Reader. You can see why I was drawn to Him. He cleaned me up quite nicely and did me well in every other way. Is it any wonder that I gave everyone else up for Him? Cling to him I do! Cling to Him I must!

Such a friend. A friend to die for! Just what my Soul needed. A fine figure and an ideal friend, coming a-bundling with packages and parcels.

He had such a nice expression on His face. He didn't sound hard-hearted or block-headed. The last thing He wanted to do was scare me off. What He did say was light, creamy, but carrying a lot of weight. I liked what He had to say and found

FRIENDSHIPS, NATURAL AND SPIRITUAL

According to Aristotle, the Greek philosopher (384–322 BC), it takes two people, each a social animal, to make a friendship, and many such friendships to make a society.

According to Cicero, the Roman lawyer and philosopher (104–43 BC), it takes two to make a friendship, but one may have more than one friendship at a time. His essay "Friendship" is a dialogue between himself and an assortment of crusty old friends.

According to Aelred of Rievaulx, Cictercian abbot and scholar (1110–1167), it still takes two to make a friendship, but three to make a spiritual friendship. Two visible, one invisible, the latter being Jesus Christ. In his essay "Spiritual Friendship," which he meant to be a commentary on Cicero's essay, he dialogues with a younger monk as they both go over Cicero's text line by line.

According to Kempis (1379/80–1471), spiritual friendship takes only two, one visible and one invisible, the Soul and the Lord. As represented in *Imitation* and in *Consolations,* spiritual friendship has all the characteristics of natural friendship, from hijinx to lojinx.

it hard to tear myself away. His conversation was nothing but consolation. He could've talked with anyone at the party, but He gave me the feeling I was the only one there.

My response to what He had to say was immediate and direct. I wanted to take up His suggestions at once and try to better myself. And I had no fear that if I didn't do what He said, I might be headed for disaster and destruction.

Please note, the friendships described so far have been between men. A sentence of C. S. Lewis's comes to mind.

"My happiest hours are spent with three or four old friends in old clothes tramping together and putting up in small pubs — or else sitting up till the small hours in someone's college rooms talking nonsense, poetry, theology, metaphysics over beer, tea, and pipes. There's no sound I like better than adult male laughter" (as quoted in the revised and expanded edition of Green and Hooper's *C. S. Lewis: A Biography* [London: HarperCollins, 1974, 2000], 170).

And yet Kempis frequently cites, even swipes, language from the Canticle of Canticles (Song of Solomon), luscious and lavish language more appropriate for a bride and groom romping about on their night of nights.

Odd insight, this. During Kempis's lifetime the great emphasis in art and spirituality was on Christ Crucified, and so was Kempis's. But somehow he managed to befriend the Very One whom he'd befouled with sin.

—W.G.

32

Telling Spiritual Stories

Pore over the Scriptures — that's where you'll find the Lord.
(John 3:39)

The Lord taught me that there were so many things to enjoy, but He also toughened me up, gave me an edge. There would be things to suffer in His Majesty's Secret Service. The cross, for example. And He also introduced me to the Holy Books, giving me the armor I'd need against the Devil's traps and troops. Particularly heroic in the continuing battle were the Holy People of both the Old and New Testaments.

He also led me around through the cave and tent territory of Egypt; that was where He invigorated and increased the monks, the eremites and cenobites who'd followed in His footsteps and made the sweet yoke of Christ credible and imitable.

All the while He taught me the spiritual stories, much as a mother nudged her child, breaking nutshells and placing the sweetmeats into my mouth. Look into these stories and learn what they mean.

Open the pages of the Prophets and Apostles, and cast your eyes on the mysteries contained therein. Unwind Isaiah, inspect the Gospel, and just see if you don't discover the sweetest fruits in them.

In these very same pages you'll almost certainly find the obscure and the difficult passage; that's to say, the meat still clinging to the nutshell. But if you hear some explanation of the passage and understand what a moment ago was a mystery, you'll find the shell broken open and the sweetmeat popped out.

So it should be when you come across sentences that are just too subtle to understand. Yes, there'll be times when that happens, but perhaps you can intuit what's inside; that's to say, the hidden meanings.

How else do you think the Lord carried me on His shoulders? Whenever He saw me fall, He could have left me behind, but He didn't. Patiently and over the long haul, He held on to me for dear life. And He inspired others to put up with my bag of tricks.

I wasn't the first load He'd carried on His shoulders. There was the cross, the one He hauled to that spot called Calvary, where He was crucified and died; John told the story in his Gospel (19:17–18). There on His shoulders were burdens more grave than my sins alone; there were the sins of all Humankind. It was because of them, not because of Himself, that He'd carried, hauled, dragged that cross.

FOR ALL THAT He deserves to be honored, loved, venerated above all else!

That's why I call him my Beloved Friend, somebody as unique to me as my mother. And I truly know that I don't deserve to be singled out and loved by Him. Nevertheless, that's how He behaved toward me. There was no earthly reason why He should've done so. If I were He, I wouldn't just run up to strangers and hug them one right after another, would you?

Remember that scene in the Old Testament when David asked, "Who am I that I should become a relative of the king?" (VUL 1 Kings 18:18; NRSV 1 Samuel 18:18). And David's degree of affinity was greater by far than mine. But the Lord's choice of me was a pure and chaste one — an echo from Peter's First (3:16). Flesh and Blood had nothing to do with it. God is Charity, and such Charity gives birth to thoughts like this. John, the disciple whom Jesus liked a lot, had this to say in his First Letter. "The greater one is the one who's in us rather than the one who's in the world" (4:4, 8).

THE LORD did it to David, relative of an earthly king, and the Lord of Lords did it to me, raised us both from the lesser to the greater.

I mean, He just did it, swooped down and swept me up; it wasn't as though I'd done something to deserve it. Whatever was going through His mind at the time, I have no idea; He just thought it worth His while. It just seemed to chuckle His Charity and tickle his Infinite Goodness no end.

Soul so happy, Soul so blessed, kiss the chain that ties you to Divine Love.

How noble and how freeborn not to notice the vows that link you to Him.

Alas, my tall tale about my Beloved Friend has gone on for far too long. That's not to say there isn't a great deal more to tell. But that'll be another story told by another person at another time. And that'll be the Lord Himself, who once thought it nice to do a little something for me.

33

Surviving Temptation

The mischievous maid knows where her mistress is at all times.
I wish I could do as well with my mischievous Friend.

(Psalm VUL 122:2; NRSV 123:2)

From the very first moment, the Lord and I hit it off, dear Reader, and I wanted to make the relationship last. So I promised to do a few things; He did the same. "Stick with Me," He said, "and I'll stick with you, and who knows what wonderful things will happen?" (John 15:5).

As with all relationships, it had to be tested. In this case, testing meant temptation. Of course, that meant temptation for me, not for my new Friend.

Needless to say, there were some benefits from temptation that I hadn't thought of before, like roughing up the interior man, making a fallow spiritual life fruitful, getting a better idea of just what spiritual gifts were. That having been said, Temptation — she grabbed me and threw me to the ground. Not once, but again and again! And from that moment on my Soul was in continuous pain.

My Divine Friend was in the room at the time, and He knew what was going on in my heart. He knew it wasn't a figment of my imagination or some passing fancy. When I was depressed with anxiety to the point where I didn't believe

I'd survive, He helped me. As the Psalmist encouraged me to believe, if He didn't help me, then my Soul would've enjoyed the tortures of the Damned (VUL 93:17; NRSV 64:17).

Yes, He felt sorry for me. But then again He always seemed to show up for a heart that needed Him. Who else could've gotten the upper hand when it came to tolerating so many temptations unless God Himself was protecting and helping him out? When I realized all this, I could finally stand facing Heaven.

Of course up to that point I'd never put my faith in anything but the living flesh. I may've been naive, but I never thought that, because the heavens appeared serene, there was some guarantee of security. Suddenly, without warning, dust devils blew up. That's when I needed the Grace and Protection of my Beloved Friend, facing almost everything in the world as a booby trap. No place was safe, except perhaps Heaven, where my Beloved Friend dines in joy and exaltation with His best friends.

WAS THERE SOMETHING ELSE I was supposed to do? Should I have planned out a course of action? Shouldn't my Beloved Friend have mapped out an intermediate plan? I mean, couldn't He have come and picked me up and placed me down in a lovely meadow, a place where Saints were larking about and Devils weren't lurking around.

Instead, great storms of temptation rose up with the winds every which way, leaving me laboring to stay afloat, doubting that I'd ever reach the port of Salvation alive.

ALAS, DEAR READER, nothing I do can guarantee my plucking success from failure, but I do have a short list of things I've found helpful. I've always managed to survive because . . .

I always see the light of faith.

I admit to my Beloved Friend that I need His Grace.

I never let go of His Charity.

I put my trust in Him before I put it in myself.

When I fail, fall into a vice, I immediately let out a howl for Him, stammering a prayer like the following.

"My Lord and my God, have mercy on my Soul! Don't let me venture into a field of temptations again. Help me to fight back and overcome all hardship. Give me Your hand — no, not the left one, that's where Satan is — the right one!"

That last bit was Job's, and he should've known (14:15).

34

Benefiting from Temptation

*Having survived temptation,
the person will receive the Crown of Life Award,
promised by the Lord to those who love Him.*

(James 1:12)

When temptation comes, dear Reader, I holler my head off.
But when temptation overwhelms me, I can't holler at all. All
I can do is take deep breaths.

The Lord knows the things hidden in my heart, as the
Psalmist has said (VUL 43:22; NRSV 44:21). He knows what
the Spirit desires, as Paul wrote to the Romans (8:21). For
Him it's out of the question that one of His little ones should
die the death, as Matthew the Evangelist noted (18:16).

His Mercy is always with me, even though I fail to notice
it; indeed even though I failed to notice Him administering
it. Yes, apparently He's always with me, always preventing me
from surrendering myself to my passions.

The Lord has promised that I will win the war against
Temptation. If that's so, how come I lose so many of the
skirmishes, the small vices creeping and crawling all over me
and tying me down? Perhaps this isn't such a bad thing after
all. I do have this tendency to puff myself up in my own eyes,
to presume that I'm the Lord High and Mighty.

To be humble and to learn to handle my obfuscation — I have to learn that by myself alone I'm nothing, I don't amount to a hill of beans.

What's so funny about this is how well I look in the morning mirror, at the top of my form, that sort of thing. In truth, I'm only a hair's breadth away from complete collapse. The Genesist had something to say on that (1:5).

Dear Reader, I offer this piece of advice lest you praise me too rashly, jump too quickly to a conclusion. Yes, I may seem to be pottering along quite nicely, proceeding with all deliberate haste. But the Lord, as He did with Job, visits me each morning with a new temptation in one pocket and the way out of it in the other (7:18). Yes, it's the Lord's work, not mine. Praise Him! Often He was holding my hand. More than once when I'd been taken prisoner or hostage by the Enemy, He ransomed me handsomely.

Other times as the battle raged and the Enemy surged, He sent His arrows whipping toward the swarming hoards, multiplying His lightnings till the Enemy turned in retreat. He could've demanded my unconditional surrender, but he rarely gave that gift even to the Saints in this life, let alone to me.

AFTER ALL THIS horrific hullabaloo, I had a modest rest, some quiet time, rest and relaxation. All this through the largesse of my Beloved Friend. It took some getting used to, but I didn't get it for corporeal or secular ease. I was supposed to spend it on self-improvement, pondering the secrets of the heavens for a little while.

35

Resting between Temptations

On the seventh day you'll rest.

(Exodus 34:21)

Pay some attention to me now, dear Lord. I need to find out what kind of person I am, and what better ways I can please you. After all, You've already shown me so many signs of love. If I were to put them on the scales, they'd greatly outweigh my poor, pathetic merits.

In the turbine of temptation, dear Reader, I've often lost sight of my Beloved Friend but, in my rest and relaxation time, without a ripple on my placid mind, I see Him all too well, and we do what friends do, cling, the one to the other.

WHO WOULDN'T WANT to stand in the shadow of a Beloved Friend like that, especially when time and place permit?

I don't always have to feel a tidal wave coming, nor do I always continue to smack my lips over a personal favor.

Come evening, come morning, and we have one day, hithering and thithering through happy and sad — that's what this mortal life is all about. He'd sensed this, that wretched Job, "Surprise him at dawn! Attack him before he can shake the sleepers from his eyes! That's the Lord's strategy" (7:18).

IT'S SUCH A SHORT TIME between temptations, but I'm not complaining. The in-betweens are always long enough, good and hopeful times. When I see Him, I always give Him a ceremonious salute. Not always off to the wars, He wants to spend a festive day with me. Everything seems to make sense when He's around. Before His gaze the fog of my personal wars — that's to say, all my stupid, crazy ideas — is driven away, and in its place comes the long-hoped-for serenity.

When He enters a room, everything has to be spotless, nothing can be out of place. That, the Devils who specialize in dust have trouble with. But all my passions have to be in their proper places. They used to keep me in an uproar, disturbing the furniture, upsetting the decor. But He'd slip into the secret places of my heart right in the middle of a brawl, calming me down, driving the Devils to distraction, restoring the pieces of furniture to their upright positions!

I FEEL a prayer coming on.

"So I put it to You, my cordial, handsome Friend, admit me to Your company whenever You see me being assaulted by some unhelpful vices or amused by some unuseful occupation. Don't let me wander off in my distracted state. Remind me where my one, true hearth really is.

"You're my Lord and my God. By Your word You cleaned and sanctified all things. You diverted my feet away from the deadly traps and placed them on secured roads."

WHAT IF I'M LEFT bereft by my Beloved Friend, you ask?

What a mischievous question, dear Reader!

Well, if you must know, I try to keep myself on an even keel until He comes back. I'm worn down by Nature, but I'm buoyed up by Spirit. That prevents the pain from becoming inconsolable. I remember that Humankind can't live without love and the pain it brings.

From Faith comes life; from Scripture, belief; so said Romans (1:17), Galatians (3:11), Hebrews (10:38). From consolation comes not only ascent but also assent. And although up to this point in my life, I've done bad things, I don't have to shuffle my feet about resolving to do better, nor should I twiddle my fingers any more. Or so statements made by the Saints have led me to believe.

36

Losing a Step or Two

Everyone should be quick to listen, slow to speak,
slower still to anger.

(James 1:19)

If I've lost some of my devotion, lost a step or two in my dogged pursuit of doing good things, it's truly my loss, but a loss not without a remedy. Job had a worst case scenario. "A good and just man takes my life, but that doesn't mean there's no good left in him" (13:15).

THE WORK of acquiring Virtue is often difficult, hard to get a handle on. But the more it's tried, the easier it becomes. The same with Success; the closer you get to it, the fuzzier it becomes.

Just when you think the acquisition process has been concluded, that's precisely when you lose confidence and fall into the shredder. Be patient and commend yourself to God's Justice. The Lord isn't such a lout as to leave you disconsolate for long periods of time.

Do take care not to *mea culpa* yourself to death. Thump your breast a couple of times, yes, but don't thwack it until your heart stops. Get a hold of yourself and get a handle on your pain, even as your heart and body pull you down.

Do stick to your original plan, and do lean on your Beloved Friend as much as you can.

Wait patiently for Heavenly Consolation and, when it comes, you'll feel the Grace welling up, and the respect of God.

From the Psalmist comes a faithful scriptural citation. "He said He'd come. I waited and waited till I thought He'd never come. And then He came" (VUL 39:2; NRSV 40:1).

Pray more often than you have in the past. Pray for what you want. And pray for what you don't want, especially when He thinks it's in your better interest.

"You know you're not My only friend. I have oodles and oodles of others, and all are always clamoring for my attention every hour of every day, every day and every night," as the Psalmist might have put it (VUL 30:16; NRSV 31:15). "I get around to everyone eventually. But if you want Me to console you now, I'll spot you one on account.

"Yes, if you persevere in Patience and Longanimity, and if you don't take a dip in virtuous living every time you hit a bump in the road, the Illumination and Consolation you've been missing will return. And it'll be as though it had never left. Indeed, it'll be better."

37

Arguing with a Beloved Friend

Yes, Your works are dazzling and, yes, I have to shade my eyes!
(Psalm VUL 138:14; NRSV 139:14)

So what do you have to say for Yourself, my Far-flung Friend, now that You've returned? Answer me!

Why did You dump me and run off with someone else? I want an answer, and I want it now!

And while You're at it, you might just tell me why You came back.

Cat got Your tongue?

All I know is that, if you hadn't come back, I'd be at Death's door. So You had second thoughts. Lucky You! All I had was one thought, that I was sad You left, and now I'm glad You've come back.

So say something, anything that'll give me a clue. You must've had an excuse. Make it a good one!

Obviously, You went on to another, a better friend. Well, did You know that kicked the stuffing out of me? Sounds good to You?

So You like my story better than Yours? Well, so do I.

Don't go. Don't be flighty, like the risen Jesus in Luke (24:29). Stay the night with us, Lord. The dark is coming fast.

Come, join us Devouts. We want to hear Your story. You're a good storyteller, a smooth talker. I won't get mad. But You do owe me an explanation.

If you don't want to make excuses, then why don't You tell me who You are. Who you really are.

"So you want to know who I am," said the Lord, opening His mouth for the first time since He returned.

"Well, I'm the one in the Prophecy of Isaiah who comes speaking Justice (63:1). Who can match my Counsel and Prudence?

"Yes, I have something to do with the sea's being wet and the desert's being dry.

"I'm Watchman in Isaiah, the one who turns the lights off and then some hours later turns them back on (45:7).

"I'm Rescuer when someone takes a header into the abyss.

"I'm Reader of Hearts, Augurer of Innards, in the Psalms (VUL 7:10; NRSV 7:9).

"I'm Encyclopedist in the Psalms. I know all the latest stuff and all the oldest stuff (VUL 138:5; NRSV 139:4).

"I'm Weights and Measures in the wisdom books, and I invented all the calculations to make them work (VUL Book of Wisdom 11:21; NRSV Wisdom of Solomon 11:21).

"I'm Creator of Heaven and Earth, Grand Navigator of shoals and shallows.

"I'm Cataloger of your secrets, Revealer of your hiddenmost.

"I'm Embracer of the Universe, Hugger and Squeezer of all I can reach.

"In other words, I'm God.

"I'm God, and I don't know the meaning of the word "change.""

"I'm God, and in My bubbling presence all the brightly babbling Reasoners stand stone silent.

"I'm God, and I hold all the power. You can ignore it, flout it, complain about it, but you can't lay a finger on it.

"I'm God, and I'm the Most High. Start climbing now and by life's end you'll be no closer to the top than you are now.

"I'm God, and I'm Good. Contain me if you like, but first you'll have to find a large enough bin to put Me in.

"I'm the easiest person in the world to find, and yet I'm the easiest person to lose.

"I'm the one who nestles in your innermost heart, and yet I'm the one who wrestles in your outermost night.

"All the stuff in the world I can carry without breaking a sweat. All the people in the world I can rule without, if I may borrow some words from Paul's First to the Corinthians, 'a discouraging word' (14:3).

"I can peer into the past as well as the future, to say nothing of the present.

"My specifications exceed those of every corporal and spiritual creature, bar none.

"I'm known by many names, depending on the circumstances; and I create many things that none of you knows.

"Now you see Me, now you don't, and you haven't a clue as to why or wherefore.

"Yes, I'm the Hidden God in Isaiah (45:15), and yet I keep in constant touch with all My good friends."

HIDE-AND-SEEK

Kempis wasn't the only one in the fifteenth century writing about "the hidden God" (*Consolations,* 37). In 1445 a contemporary of his, Nicholas of Cusa (1401–1461), published an essay, *The Hidden God (De deo abscondito)*. It was a philosophical work in dialogue form that could well have been written in the twentieth century. It has all the hallmarks of *En attendant Godot (Waiting for Godot,* 1952) by Samuel Beckett, an existential play about the great eschatological wait of a ragtag group who knew they ought to wait but didn't quite know whom they were waiting for.

Written centuries before, *The Hidden God* is about two characters waiting for God, but only one of them happens to be a nonbeliever. The believer feels that while he's waiting, he ought to be doing something directionally appropriate. Here are the opening lines of Cusa's dialogue, paraphrased from the Latin original.

PAGAN. So tell me now, what are you really doing out here in the wilderness with your knickers all bunched up?

CHRISTIAN. I'm praying.

PAGAN. What's that?

CHRISTIAN. I'm lying here on the ground in a position of adoration.

PAGAN. What's that?

CHRISTIAN. It's *praying*. I'm lying here praying, paying my respects to, adoring... God.

PAGAN. Who's *God?*

CHRISTIAN. That's just it. I don't know.

PAGAN. You don't know? Then how, in all seriousness, can you adore, pay your respects to, pray to, someone you don't know?

CHRISTIAN. It's because I don't know — that's why I feel I have to adore — just to be on the safe side.

Cusa himself attended universities in Heidelberg, Padua, and Cologne, where he studied Law, Mathematics, Astronomy, Philosophy, and Theology. He was ordained a priest and spent twenty-five years in the papal diplomatic corps; near the end of his life he was made bishop and named cardinal. He's happily remembered for *ignorantia docta,* his theory that an educated person should know what he or she doesn't or can't know.

Cusa's character is a Christian intellectual who's been to university; he knows there's a God, and he knows what Philosophy and Theology say about that God. Hence, his inquiry. Yes, for him God exists, but God's beyond Philosophy, beyond Theology; so far beyond that He can't really be seen or known by a believer. So as not to give the wrong impression, Cusa's next work was "*De visione Dei*" (The Not-So-Hidden God).

Kempis's character, if I may call his Soul a character, hasn't been to university; rather he was matriculated at the school of the Soul, and as a result he has direct knowledge of God, especially of God's penchant for playing hide-and-seek.

In *Consolations* Kempis noted that God wasn't the only one playing this game. "Yes, said the Soul, I admit to playing hide-and-seek with You, Lord, and, yes, I'm still sinning my way merrily through life" (7).

Yet another varietal of the game. "Whenever you pray," Matthew recorded the Lord as saying on the Mount, "go to your room and shut the door behind you. Then pray to the Father, and He'll respond, and no one else'll be the wiser" (6:6). —W.G.

38

Titting for Tatting

Life for life, eye for eye,
tooth for tooth, hand for hand, foot for foot.

(Exodus 21:24)

So much for what the Lord said to me, dear Reader. This is what my Soul said to Him.

"You hide from me — that's why I hide from You. I'm the creature who goes into hiding whenever I lose touch with You."

"I may hide My face from you every now and then," the Lord replied, "and you know why I do it?"

"I'm almost afraid to ask."

"Because I want to know whether your love for Me is chaste."

"Just what does that mean?"

"To love Me for Myself, not for what you hope to get out of Me. Not for some temporal nicety. Not for a material perk. Not for what you can squeak out of the situation."

"Why are you telling me all this?"

"Not everybody loves Me that way. Only the most perfect soul has Love that's chaste."

UP TO THIS POINT, dear Reader, my Soul has been somewhat less than perfect, and hence it's had to prove itself, be put through its paces, that sort of thing, all the way to contempt of self, all the way to God Himself.

"Dear Lord, when I'm swanning about, up to my nose in interesting things and to a great extent involved in the joyful things of this life, I also feel that I'm filled with devotion. Don't You think so?"

"Yes, dear Soul, sometimes you're a real kick in the pants; other times, You're just a pain in the neck."

"Well, dear Lord, what an awful thing to say!"

"You do do good things, but even sinners do that," said the Lord. "As Jesus Son of Sirach put it, they bless me in as often as they bless me out (vul Ecclesiasticus 15:19; nrsv Sirach 15:19). But I mean, who wouldn't love a guy like Me for all the good things I do for them, all the consolations I bring to them. What more could a sinner hope for?"

"Well," asked the Soul of the Lord, "if You know so much, how do I make progress in the spiritual life?"

"Well," replied the Lord to the Soul, "work! You have to work at it. But you don't want to work at it, do you? You just want to sit there feeding your face with yogurt. Well, you're going to have to switch to solid food today. It's time to tear yourself away from the tit, to make room for all the tots that have yet to suckle there.

"David, it's time to join the number of the brave! Grab that spear and sword and shield of yours.

"Yes, it's time to grab hold of the cross and follow Me.

"Besides, if you want to be counted among those who've endured over the centuries, yet enjoyed many showers of grace, then it's time to get the lead out!

"Just look at yourself — soft, puffy, lethargic — waiting for Consolation to be served up to you on a platter!

"Is it any wonder I want to train you up by showing you the dark side of the spiritual life, all the suffering in the world, anything to prevent you from thinking yourself such a holy and innocent thing? Let Me tell you, and you can find it in the Psalms, you can expect such an attack as could only be launched against you by Hell's Angels (VUL 77:49; NRSV 78:49).

"Some of these dark creatures will be right in your face, trying to drag you under the bushes. Some will treat you like a draft animal. Some will lead you where you don't want to go. Some will assail you on the outside; others from the inside. Some will lead you to the podium to accept honors and the status that goes with them; yet the only honor and status you deserve are harsh words and hard labor. But worse is yet to come. It's to Hell and back for you. After all, you'll have to prove once and for all that you're an athlete running in My race.

"HAVE NO FEAR. I won't take off points, and I won't add points, until I've examined you thoroughly. Why? To see if you really did what you said you did or were just faking it. This is your Beloved Friend talking. I want you to answer Me the way the Bride in the Canticles would; that's to say, as though you really wanted to set up your own private getaway with me.

"YOU MAY COME to the conclusion that this discipline isn't as lovable in fact as it is in theory — I'm speaking now of your slobbering all over the place during My absence when you should've been tracking Me down with Affection and Perseverance.

"Of course, if you feel right off you don't have the right stuff, then I'll send you my staff, something to lean on, as you try to get up, raise yourself to your full height.

"Yes, I'll forgive you and, yes, I'll return you to your baptismal state.

"Yes, dear Soul Friend, you're right after all. I'm the one who's the softy. It's just I'm unwilling to conclude that you or anybody else is a total flop. Why? Because you're a friend, and that's what friends do.

"Even if your love is still not as perfect as you or I would like, I'm not going to tromp all over you. In fact, I'm going to do just the opposite. I'm going to pick you up and dust you off, and I'm going to help you grow. I'm putting you under My personal care until you do well again, until you stop clinging to Me and stand up on your own. Something, of course, that'll never happen.

"Yes, I know what your threshhold of suffering is, so I'll adjust the flow of ruinations to suit you. I don't want you bearing up bravely only to be crushed by the sheer weight of them. What kind of a fool would I be then?"

39

Readjusting
the Schedule

We're on different timetables, you and I.
(John 7:6)

Not now, but soon.
(John 13:36)

I'm uncertain of my schedule, said the Lord to the Soul; do wait for me. Even if it takes Me to the Day of Visitation, I'll come again. Probably long before then, and that's a promise.

In the meantime, get serious about prayer, read the Holy Book and, in everything that comes down the pike, hold your course as though your life depended on it.

Just don't ignore the fact that much of your spiritual journey is grunt and grind; don't fall victim to the trudge.

Do know that the last thing I want to hear from you while I'm away is excuses. *Oh I'm so sick, and it came upon me so suddenly that I think I'm going to die, and I don't want to die alone, and why is there never a doctor when you need one!* That sort of thing just doesn't please Me at all.

Where's your faith, man? You have to have great faith in this enterprise. When you don't see Me, you should see yourself and all the things you believe in.

Yes, you do ignore My judgments from time to time. That's when Faith, stunning in her firmness, speaks up, "What a relief that God's running the whole show!"

That's how I'll console you. Don't worry, that infirmity you suffer from, it'll drive you crazy, but it won't kill you; on the contrary it'll lead you to the glory of God.

Yes, I have to admit, one time I deliberately took away your desire. I wanted to try your Faith and Love. Yes, I did that, that and other things, if only to show how weak you really are.

Yes, I've known you and all things before the cuckoo in the clock clucked for the first time. Therefore, acknowledge that what you know about the spiritual life comes from Me. About the best you could do on your own was become a poor pauper.

That's not to say you haven't made some progress in self-knowledge, but you must make more. That's why I give you a kick in the pants every now and then. It's not a bad thing, you know, to be down in the dumps every once in a while. You're troubled, you're humbled, but that's the only way for you to appreciate the proper infirmity assigned to you.

"YOU'RE REALLY QUITE ARROGANT," said the Lord, continuing His rant, "did you know that? You don't seem to possess any self-knowledge. You think you possess a good you don't really have. You're awash with self-love, without a thought in the world as to who gave you the gift, you abuse the very gift itself.

"You found Me intoxicating, but you forgot the tillage and toilage it took to produce the cluster of grapes that produced the wine in this most excellent cup. Admit that all your resources are spent. Admit also that your next best chance to survive comes from above.

"Give therefore the honor that's due to Grace. Admit that without Me you can do nothing. Consider how totally dependent you are on Me. Where were you before I looked you up? Nowhere, except up to your nose in sin.

"That was then, but where have you got to now? Nowhere at all if I hadn't been leading you by the nose. But when things went well with you, didn't I have a hand in it?"

"Yes, sweetest Lord," I replied. "You had a finger in my pudding right from the start."

"When, dear Soul, did you first think that things between you and Me weren't going well? That you could get a better deal elsewhere? So what did I do that was so wrong? Did my glory and praise of your promise in the spiritual life fall short? Did you no longer like the look of me?"

"No, Dear Lord, it was never that. There's no one like You in pulchritude and beatitude, in wealth and power, and that includes in Heaven or on Earth.

"For You're the sole most high, there's no one else, over all creatures. Yours are the Heavens; yours, the Earth — the Psalmist couldn't have put it better (VUL 88:12; NRSV 89:11). The orb of the earth and the plenitude You founded Yourself. Much You've given to the Created World, and from it great pulchritude and wisdom and goodness are reflected. But all their lights taken together are as shadows of your Blessed and Glorious Presence. All this I've learned by experience, the bitter experience of Your having left me — shades of Jeremiah (2:19)!

PUT YOUR HOPE and faith in me, said the Lord to the Soul, not only for the Day of Visitation, but even more so for the Night of Temptation, that is to come.

I sent you off the sooner so you'd return the sooner in a heap; that's to say, after you'd tasted the sweets the world had to offer — sour balls and all!

My love has lightened your life. How many times did you find it inviting?

Now I did take into account that you didn't have a perfectly good excuse when you left, that you were just bored to tears, weary with temptations, whipped from pillar to post with afflictions. That there was no one who'd give you counsel, that help was nowhere to be found, that only a crimped and cramped life awaited you.

That's why I leave you, that you may acknowledge My presence by My absence. In small things and large. In near places and far. In early times and late. Wherever you are, go settle.

Yes, you walk with your Beloved Friend again, yes, but with fear, anxiety, humility in your heart, as the prophet Micah put it (6:8). Yes, you must abstain from vain things, and avoid committing offenses. Yes, I leave you so that you'll come to know how much you love Me.

You used to think yourself a pretty formidable person and more blessed than you actually were. But it's now more evident that, once I'd pulled back a little, you lost it all and were totally wretched.

But how could you learn to love until you'd gotten used to carrying around the weight of it all? Where was I during all this? Like the lover in the Canticles, I was just leaning against a wall, an interested third party (vul 2:9; nrsv Song of Solomon 2:9), but I was watching you break a sweat, turning red with the effort, hotting up the old fervor.

One look at you, and I know everything.
If you love Me, you won't be slow to search.
If I please you, you can just go search for Me.

SURELY YOU KNOW — or don't you? — that the value of a commodity, any commodity, spiritual or material, is directly related to the amount of labor put into it. That would apply to the weary person who finally found repose. And to the bloke disappointed in love whose love was finally returned. And to the treasure once lost and now found — in the scriptural case that had twice the value. Double the joy and twice the joyfulness with the Beloved making a special guest appearance from time to time.

And so to conclude, dear Soul, there's always a useful reason why what happens in My absence doesn't really devalue My presence.

And, I admit, I do give Myself a sort of pious dispensation to absent myself.

Dear Soul, and I hope you'll agree, vanishing every now and then suggests a certain playfulness as one might find among friends of long acquaintance.

So that's enough of an explanation.

Some secrets.

Even in your darkest you deserved a tiddle.

I grant you license to return to Me as many times as seems necessary.

If you pray in a serious and humble way, I'll make sure My door is always open to you.

Always!

40

Feeding the Flame

Yes, I've taken up with the Lord. No, I haven't lost my mind.

(Psalm VUL 58:18; NRSV 59:17; Isaiah 50:7)

"So, Lord," said the Soul, "what's so absurd about my remembering our time together? After all, You took a slug like me and hauled me up to the heights of prayer and meditation. Of course, I'm thankful!

"Yes, I know our time together is open to unfavorable interpretation. *You don't really fear God. He just happened to find you creeping and crawling with sin and felt pity for you, as though you were a slug He'd stepped on.* That sort of thing.

"So, Beloved Friend, what do You have to say to that? I'd respond myself, but who'd believe me? Sinners are mouthing off against me; the Psalmist described the problem (VUL 108:2; NRSV 109:2). Besides, even if my Soul were clean as a whistle, how would I know? I'm so confused!"

The Beloved Friend replied.

"So what if people denounce you in public! The Psalmist didn't care (VUL 68:20; NRSV 19:19). Suppose they do think you just another crazy. Why should you care? Job didn't (9:20–21). I'm the only One you have to listen to. The real reason why I came down, as you very well know, wasn't to pal around with the Just. It's the sinners, Stupid — that's what I'm quoted in Mark as saying — they're my fatal attraction" (2:17).

"Well, Lord, are You now going to tell me that I can't do what I want? But who's going to stop me, stand in my way? Who's going to call it a sin (John 8:16)? Who's going to toss the first stone (John 8:7)? For that matter, who's without sin? Who hasn't stepped in a puddle from time to time?"

"So, sinners there are, but this is what I don't understand. Why would their need for Grace detract from the divine supply of grace? Let's get one thing straight here. You didn't choose Me. I chose You. And if I want to give you or anyone else a kick in the pants to get you going, that's My business. Is that clear?"

"Quite clear," said the Soul.

"So," asked the Lord, adjusting His voice downward, trying to appear indifferent, "are people really murmuring against Me?

"No," said the Soul, "but they're *shouting* against you!"

"Well, I do like to hang with sinners, share a meal with them, that sort of thing. And the sinners don't seem to mind. They're happy when I show up and sad when I shove off."

"Lord, there's no need to look at the sins of others. I've done more than my share. I've committed more than I can count."

"Dear Soul, I know I'm kicking the stuffing out of you, but I'm doing it for your own good. Furthermore, you're not a castoff, not a throwaway. Just because you're a sinner with more defects than measles, that doesn't mean you shouldn't do something about them. I know you're depressed about it, but it's not to die for. For one thing, just count the many sinners who've turned into My closest friends.

"Yes, I'm drawn to sinners; they're the humble folk by and large. But I'm very quick to dump those who take on spiritual airs, who feel their behavior hasn't been all that bad.

"I don't make a big thing of it really when you give something of yourself to Me. Just loving Me, even with an impure, ramshackle cluttered heart — that does it every time."

"Lord, I'm embarrassed when You want to build a bonfire in me, and I can't rouse a spark."

"Dear Soul, what the Literati and Glitterati of this world demand is flash. Yet a warm, even glow from your hearth is more to my taste. Trouble is, I suppose, You're the one who has to keep feeding the flame.

41

Wiping the Slate Clean

Seven times? Seven times seventy is more like it!
(Matthew 18:21)

Dear Soul, you're habitually in bad shape. I have every right to bring you low. I've compiled a list — and a long list it is — of your infirmities and your less-than-decorous behaviors. Moan and groan all you want, but you have no legal claim on My grace, at least at the present moment.

You've been a sinner since you were a child. A cracked and clouded mirror, if I may borrow some words from the wisdom literature (VUL Book of Wisdom 7:21; NRSV Wisdom of Solomon 7:21). Just don't forget your fragile condition. Or My generous disposition. Of course you can come to Me, any time you want, confident that I won't take a swing at you, but do so only with a reverent heart.

Remember, for breakfast every morning I have *Irreverence on Toast*. Yes, I'm always the one who fills up the Impious Person with Piety when he's a quart low (Isaiah 43:26). And I sign my name on the chit, approving for destruction all the sins and derelictions of the world. And that's all I've done for now.

But now I'm prepared to offer even more mercy. Why? Because I prefer to be remembered as a Merciful Rascal, not as an Irascible Wretch. No, I don't get My jollies by punishing sinners but by saving them from the lash. You know from experience, dear Soul, that I'm never so content with a first coat of Grace that I don't apply a second and a third. And what's more, in the future I don't foresee a limit to my commiserations. There just isn't a number or a numeral high enough to put the lid on what I propose to do.

DEAR LORD, You've got my attention. Sins, forgiveness of sins, penance after sins — it's good for my complexion. My sad, solemn face begins to regain its color, joy flushing my cheeks, grace flooding my veins.

DEAR SOUL, such a sinner I'll gladly welcome into My company. Grace and praise will pervade our conversations, and if a transgression of yours pops up in the conversation, you won't have to bolt from the room. All the old wrongs are in the junk pile, wrote Paul in his Second to the Corinthians, and all the slates have been wiped clean (5:17).

People should remember I have a pious and merciful heart. I'm more prepared to forgive than you to forget. So what are you afraid of? Why are you quaking in your boots, soiling your trousers, afraid to come forward and shake my hand?

Answer Me this, if you will. Why do you go to the trouble of alienating yourself from My grace when it didn't cost you a cent in the first place?

Suppose I did impose a ceiling on my extravagance with sinful souls; that shouldn't bring your praying to a screeching halt. Nor should you lose the confidence that airing out the soul brings. Indeed, you should pray with even greater warmth, devote yourself with even greater vigor to the task at hand.

No one can verify the outside number of My commiserations. At one time no one could agree; at another time, everyone was shrugging his shoulders, piously agreeing to whatever number was put forward, however outrageous.

42

Approaching the Throne

No need to hang back. Let's approach the Throne with confidence.

(Hebrews 4:16)

Suppose, dear Soul, I turn My face to you in casual conversation and suddenly give you what your heart desires. What was it the Psalmist said? "Approach me, and your complexion will take on a glow, a warmth. No need to blush anymore" (VUL 33:6; NRSV 34:5).

More often than not I'm criticized, not for the frequency, but for the infrequency of My comings and goings. They point the accusing finger more often at My bashfulness than at My finger beckoning them to punishment. When all is said and done, put your trust in My goodness. That's the hallmark of humility and faith.

DEAR SOUL, sin no more. But if you should happen to sin, don't despair, stay off the ledge, don't jump off the bridge. Just keep your hope dry. And, if all else fails, you have Me as legal advocate before the Father; that's what My beloved John wrote in his first letter (2:1).

DEAR SOUL, I know you want to approach Me, but when? Are you going to wait until you feel worthy enough? How long do you think that'll take? Who then does have a right to enter the throne room? If only the Good and the Worthy, the Great and the Perfect, the Gentlemen and the Gentlewomen may approach me, then where should the Sinners and the Publicans queue up? That's what the evangelist Luke wanted to know (15:1).

DEAR LORD, doesn't the Gospel say that Sinners and Publicans had no trouble in approaching Jesus; or at least in getting close enough to hear what He was saying?

So, DEAR SOUL, what can I say? Let the Undeserving approach. Give them access. That's the only way they'll become worthy. For that matter let the Downright Evil have access and, before you know it, they'll become good. Same for the Insignificant and the Imperfect, that they may become Significant and Perfect. In fact, just throw the keys away. Let everyone in, and I'll shake hands with each and every human being. Drinks galore from the Living Font!

Yes, I'm the Font of Life — who can drink me dry?

Not the Desert Rat with a burning thirst.

Not the Penniless who lust for coins of any kind.

Not the Sick unto Death who want to be cured.

Not the Tepid who think their hearts will never glow again.

Not the Timid who are afraid to ask for comfort.

The Terminally Sad will be consoled.

The Arid will bloom again.

Those worn down by repetition will find their tread again.

So, dear Soul, what if anything of Humankind really tickles my fancy? That's easy — the children — just to be with them. The kindly old Proverbialist knew that (8:31).

Those among them who desire to better themselves will find Wisdom in My teaching.

The Filthy Rich ought to be more than willing to accept eternal and incorruptible riches.

Those who hunt for honors ought to be astonished when they inherit the Eternal Name in Heaven.

Happiness in Heaven will happen to the Hapless on earth.

Whoever wants a piece of the pie will come to see Me as the *Summum Bonum,* the Master Baker, the Patissier without peer.

Yes, I'll replace all temporal goods with eternal goods in Heaven.

No, I won't fail to make good on My promises but on one condition: the complete and satisfactory observance of all My commands.

The person who can do that will be gloriously crowned in Heaven for all the legitimate battling he or she had to do on this earth; at least that's what Paul wrote in his Second to Timothy (2:5).

43

Telling the Tall Tale

May the meditation of my heart meet the pleasure of Your gaze!
(Psalm VUL 18:15; NRSV 19:14)

Dear Reader, what can be more pleasant, more instructive, than meditating on our Beloved Friend for an hour? Each of us, of course, has a relationship with the Friend of Friends. Beatific Vision isn't required; earth vision will do quite nicely. Here's how it works.

First, you can recall Him from a previous visit.

Better yet, you can find Him in the pages of Scripture, lurking in the tropes and figures as well as roaming around the narrative.

Now I must say, the image you get of our Beloved Friend is far from perfect. Rather fuzzy in the center; rather sharp around the edges. Fading in, then fading out. But it's the best one can do under the circumstances.

It's hard to keep that image in one's mind for any length of time. It'll surely fade unless the Soul who loves God does something to keep it sharp. In a sense it's ebbing and flowing like the tide. That's because the vision of God, the beatitude of it, is no longer tidal; it's a pond; ripples maybe, but never a tide again.

This is the beatitude the Soul seeks; an appetite, a hunger, an attraction. Once satisfied, it has a satisfying and quieting effect. Some good things on earth have a similar effect, but far less intense.

Frequent retrospection reveals just how far a Soul may have wandered from celestial beatitude. If one could measure such things, periods of time not devoted to the pursuit of the Divine would equal periods of unhappiness and disquiet; that's to say, prolonged stretches of time in which all the feathers are ruffled and none can be smoothed. The only remedy for the Vagabond Soul is to return to His Maker, Purveyor of all Beatitude.

OF COURSE, DEAR READER, this comes as no surprise to me, nor did it to the Psalmist (VUL 102:5 and 106:9; NRSV 103:5 and 107:9). The Lord's the One who created the Soul, so He's the One who satisfies the Soul, covering him with affection, enjoying his company, and having an all-around good time.

So, dear Soul, don't just stand there. Stop gawking and forge ahead. Onward and upward. Ascend to Him who made you! Remember, you've already received the invitations. Engraved. Hand-delivered. Well, not by Angels, but almost as good. Your desires, the ones He sent you on a regular basis — they were the messy messengers.

All these tidbits of advice having been received, steel yourself to continue the trudge. Walk faster when you see Him up ahead; make up your mind to please Him when you overtake Him. Do what you have to do. One thing is sure; you must get rid of the junk lurking within.

DON'T WORRY about getting lost. You wouldn't have a chance in the world of finding Him if He hadn't already left behind a careful trail.

If your Soul languishes on a lazy vine, don't blame the Eternal Sun. But if the summer wind thaws the arctic ice, do expect your Soul to come to a boil, the lamp in your spiritual hideaway to increase its light.

The Soul prays.

True Son and True Sun, rekindle fiery hearts, rid the earth of its sadness, and lessen the labor of its work. Convert long stretches in poverty into lingering consolations.

Wonder Drug of the Sad and Tearful! Bright Lamp for the Wanderers and Seekers! Give me enough torch, but don't give my position away to the Enemy. Find me a nice hideaway and furnish it until You've readied my room in Your Mansion.

How freely I can turn to You now! How freely I can renounce everything now, with the result that I may deserve to be consoled with your Grace. Perhaps even with a glance at Your face. Yes, You never leave the Soul inconsolate for long. Consolation on earth is nice, but in Heaven, it's out of this world!

Therefore, dear Reader, be on your best behavior. Prove that you used His Graces and Consolations wisely. Show Him that in picking you to join His company of friends He made a good choice. And in return He knows just the right Consolations to send you in your moments of extreme anxiety.

Living with Him or at least close by, you'll never be more than a few minutes away. And the closer you are, the sweeter and happier it'll be for you.

So that's the situation, dear Reader. Remove yourself from it, and it'll be a tragedy. That's to say, you'll have missed a great opportunity. Note that your Friend won't be at a loss; already He has more friends than He knows what to do with. And His pulchritude shines on undiminished without so much as a blip or a bleap when you wander off into the wilderness. And then where will you be? Missing His goodness, but He won't be missing yours. So you'll be better off hanging around with Him. If you do take off again, He won't feel a bit of regret. Add a friend, lose a friend, it makes no difference to Him. And He's the only creature about whom this can be said.

O, DEAR READER, if I only had enough talent to tell this story, I'd write it down in an instant. But it's a tall, untellable tale. Which is another way of saying that it's a story not meant to be told.

It's an unthinkable story. It's the product, not of human imagination or ingenuity, but divine. It's too incredible to be believed. But what are we to make of the few shreds of story about the Creator and the Created that have come to light? Make them a remembrance of His smooth creative touch. That'll be a solace. And that'll just have to do until He shows His face in the Kingdom.

44

Complaining about
Lack of Progress

Out of sight, out of mind — that's what I'm afraid of, Lord!
(Psalm VUL 30:23; NRSV 31:22)

When You speak, Lord, my heart has ears. But now it's my turn to speak, and I hope You'll listen.

I know I'm not supposed to keep a grievance hidden from You. So why do I, like Isaiah, keep going over and over the bitterness I find in my soul (38:17), as if You didn't know it already. You, Lord, are eating my soul alive! You don't understand, do You? You haven't the foggiest why I'm saying this. That's why I don't blush when I complain with the Prophet.

To You, my Lord God, I speak. To You all things are known. You gave me the wherewithal to prevent my swanning around more than I should or my being thought an expert by the Insipid, those who have no judgment whatsoever. And it's all Your fault!

Talking to somebody so far above my social station as to give me a nosebleed — that's what hanging with You has done for me. Of course, since You know everything there is to know, it doesn't really matter what I say.

And what solace do You think should come to a person like me, who's spent so much of his life at the bottom of a barrel?

Therefore, the only way I can make headway on this is to start listening to sermons about You that are good and sweet. But when I can't see You in person, though present You may very well be, I break down in a good sob. Sure I know You're somewhere, but You're not here. Is this what You call a sign of love? I suppose You'd also call it bittersweet. But since when is the absence of something bittersweet?

Now at last the sense of the versicle at the beginning of this chapter begins to appear to me. It's rightly written of a Soul rightly loving. That's to say, there's no such thing as a cold word, at least not to a red-hot lover, nor is the ear deaf when the heart refuses to listen. The loving and well-kindled heart would know. That's to say, as long as the heart fans the flame within itself, acting as its own bellows out of the love of eternal peace.

These things the Soul says to You, Lord.

THE LORD RESPONDS but, speaking to the Soul within, adopts a softer style than usual; that's to say, more by kissing up than mouthing off.

"So what," expostulated the Lord, "if I'm the source of all your bitterness, the pill you can't swallow, the straw that breaks your back!" Again an echo of Isaiah (38:17).

"If you're going to get uppity about a little thing like My absence, then you can have it back. I'll return your peace of mind and soul, no questions asked. I just don't have the time to sit around and listen to you boohooing like a lonesome dove. I've got other, more important things to worry about.

"Like what?" demanded the Soul.

"Like the fallen state of the world!"

"Not so quick there!" said the Soul in a rush to recover lost ground.

"I must admit I haven't been myself lately. I've made some bad commitments, and hence my contemplation has suffered. I should be sad and anxious about this state of affairs, but I hardly have the strength for it. I've lost my bearings. I don't know really where I am.

"But now that You're talking to me again, Lord, I feel better, less jumbled. Keep it up, and I wouldn't be surprised if I once again turn toward eternal things. Who'd've thought? No, I'm not already enjoying celestial goodies and, yes, I'm still being crucified by the evils of the world, but I'm bitching and moaning less."

"Does anything I've said make sense to you?" asked the Lord.

"Not to me, it doesn't. That's why I cry out to You, Lord, not with my own words, but with these words from Paul to the Romans. 'I'm such a poor, unhappy bloke! Will no one spring me from this corporeal deathtrap?' (7:21).

"Yes, flapping around in this body has been a heavy burden. No need to make it worse by wandering off into the desert, leaving behind all sorts of Consolation, and to find what? No, I want to labor along in love with You, my Beloved Friend, whether present or absent, with only You as Consolation, regular or random.

"It's as plain as the nose on my face, Lord. I can't be satisfied with the ragdolly goods of this world, although I love them dearly; only with the waxdolly goods of the next world — the sort that I can only assume are already gracing my future accommodations in the Heavenly Mansion."

TEARS AS PURGATORY

Cry me a river — that's what the Lord seems to be saying to the Soul, and what Kempis in *Consolations* seems to be saying to the Reader.

Crying, mourning sins that one's committed, is a purgatorial exercise intended to wipe away whatever temporal punishment may be due to sin, a cleansing process before one can be welcomed into Heaven. Kempis proposed in virtually all of his writings that it'd be better all around if a Christian chose to do his purgatorial time in this world rather than the next. He wasn't the first to urge this, and certainly not the last, but few did it more vigorously. Of course he had the full support of the Hebrew and Greek Scriptures.

Job did it. "The tears came. My face went all a-blubber, my eyelids shaded out the light" (VUL 16:17; NRSV 16:16).

The Psalmist did it. "Hear me, O Lord, when I cry out!" (VUL 28:7; NRSV 27:7). There were tears in his eyes, but strength in his cries.

Isaiah did it. "I joined Jazer in weeping for the loss of the vines; I drowned you with my tears" (16:9).

Jeremiah did it. "Make my head a fountain, and tears'll flow from my eyes. Then I'll be able to cry me a river whenever I want" (9:1).

Mary Magdalen did it. She, or another woman with the same name, washed the Lord's feet with her tears; He commented on her love, forgave her her sins, and sent her off with a blessing (Luke 7:36–50).

Jesus Himself did it. His tearful yet manful cries in the Garden of Gethsemane were heard in Heaven; His father especially appreciated the respect and reverence in his Son's voice; at least according to Hebrews (5:7).

So much for tears as an integral, essential element in any healthy spiritual life. Practically speaking, literary and theological types have tended to produce pictures of Purgatory, and consumers over the centuries have been wisely, but sometimes wildly, entertained by them.

Patrick (flourished fifth century), patron saint of Ireland, during his working days on earth discovered a cave on the island of Loch Derg, off the coast of western Ireland. An entrance to Purgatory, it was revealed to him, or so the legend had it. Reluctant would-be converts were led there and offered either a Purgatory on earth or a Purgatory after death.

Dante Alighieri (1265–1321) in his *Purgatorio,* one of the three parts of his *Divina Commedia,* pictured Purgatory as a sort of Guggenheim Museum; that's to say, an ascending spiral, passing ever higher through seven tiers or floors, each one devoted to one of the capital sins — Pride, Avarice, Lust, Envy, Glutton, Anger, Sloth — a compendium of all sins, really. As narrator and friends wend their purgative journey upward, their tattered filthy togs are cleansed of the offending stains; buoying their spirits is the thought that at the top, their baptismal togs having been returned to their pristine whiteness, they'll have a vision of the Heavenly Jerusalem.

In *The Canterbury Tales,* Geoffrey Chaucer (1345–1400), taking as his cue the great Augustine, bishop of Hippo, who proposed an intimate connection between salvation by fire and fiery marital intercourse, created a character who thought the same: Justinus in "The Merchant's Tale," whose own marriage certainly hadn't proved to be Heaven on earth.

Yes, this was Purgatory as perceived by a few others up to Kempis's time. But I doubt that a better portrait of that purgatorial place has been done since Kempis's own.

"A quiet, decent, penitential sort of place where I may weep for my sins" (*Consolations,* 2). —W.G.

45

Gushing Holy Tears

Tears everywhere, drenching the bed, soaking the sofa.
(Psalm VUL 6:7; NRSV 6:6)

Yes, my Soul loves recklessly, keeps the flame high. Located in
the body as it is, it's capable of contemplation and does indeed
contemplate. Nonetheless, its insatiable affection for creatures
and created things perseveres, no matter what. Happily, it'll
stop once the body is buried. Thus ends my earthly journey.
Thus begins my heavenly journey.

A PRAYER.
  *O King of Heaven, Great, Lovable, Desirable! When will I
get the joy of seeing You face to face? My soul cries out to You
because You haven't come! As long as I live on earth, I won't see
you! Sounds like I'm writing the sad psalms again. When will I
come and appear before the face of my God? (Psalm VUL 41:3;
NRSV 42:2)*
  *"I cry during the day, and I can't seem to stop throughout the
night," as the Psalmist put it, leaving me with one thought, and
one thought only. Where's my God?*

DEAR SOUL, said the Lord, there's nothing wrong with you if
and when you weep for Me *in absentia.* In trying times like

these, though, do realize that you're being fed and comforted more than in sumptuous times.

THE LOVER'S SPECIAL DEVOTION is a gush of holy tears.

Tears are for those who are strung together out of miserable necessity. One person because he's sick, another because he's oppressed, another one because he suffers from an injury, still another who's lost his will and cries about the hopelessness of it all.

Only you, my devout Soul, pour out the tears of Divine Love. For temporal injuries and transitory causes, you submit yourself to the true judgment of God and give thanks.

No one's so undevout as to judge you insipid or impatient when they hear you crying in such a state. That's because the tears aren't so depressing. They're not the kind that stain; rather they're the kind that clean. They're not the kind that blur the eyes; rather they increase the sight of the eyes of the heart.

Let them think about you, good or ill, what they will. I can't think anything but good about you, and I desire to drink deep from a similar well of tears.

I CRY ALONE, but He wants to cry with me. Is that Consolation or what?

GOD EXISTS. I know it. I believe it. It'd be easier to deny that Heaven and Earth don't exist than to deny the existence of God.

God exists, and He's the good of my Soul, and I can never become happy without His thinking it first.

Yes, His contemplation hasn't been brought to me yet, nor has it been firmed up by You eternally. And so perhaps I'm making too much of a fuss. So what if I find myself up the dark alleys of life. That's why I've been hit over the head with an appropriate infirmity. Supposedly, Celestial Glory, which I spend so much time meditating on, is just a hoax, put together with smoke and mirrors.

WHEN IT'S TIME for me to chant the Divine Office in the chapel, I often intone the dirge. Why? Because every moment of every day I'm tormented by the question, "Where's God?" It drove the Psalmist mad (VUL 41:4; NRSV 42:3)! It's driving me out of my mind! I just don't know where I stand. Where's the perfect Joy of my heart? Where's Peace and True Repose? Not on earth, only in Heaven — I know that already. But here I am, stuck here on earth, with no relief in sight.

ABOUT MY ENDLESS QUESTIONS, here's a roundup.

Where's my God whom I so love but don't yet see? Whose love for me is so great that it causes a wound in my side? Him who was seen once and taught everything?

Where's my God, whom my heart and flesh want to joyfully join in exaltation?

Where's my God for whom I sustain so many labors and dolors? Whose memory is sweet but presence dearer when it comes to repelling all gloominess from the heart?

Where's my hope? Isn't it in You, God, whom I hope to face one day?

Show Your glory, and don't turn Your face from me. Then I'll stop bitching and moaning.

IF I DISPUTE with You like a lawyer, Lord, You'll reproach me for going too fast. But I can't help it. Besides, I like all the tropes and figures. But You force me to wait, cool my heels, that sort of thing. Odd, though. Waiting itself is dangerous in that it stimulates me to complain even more. Yes, it's become something of a lovers' duel.

TEARS AS GIFT

Tears, yes, but are they real tears, or crocodile tears?

In answer, I defer to John Climacus (died A.D. 649), monk and abbot of the monastery on Mt. Sinai. In his monastic treatise entitled *The Ladder of Divine Ascent* (*The Stairway to Paradise*), he distinguished three types of tears.

Natural tears such as those aroused by anger, jealousy, frustration.

Natural tears such as those prompted by loss, pain, bereavement, compassion.

Supranatural, or supernatural, tears, which are the sort of tearage that the mystics and scholars of mysticism speak of when they talk about the "gift of tears."

Oddly enough, tears not only represent sadness at something precious that has been lost but, in moderation, they also bring about healing and eventually joy.

On the importance of tears to a healthy spiritual life, Isaac of Nineveh (seventh century), whose writings have been not unfavorably compared with those of Kempis, had this to say.

"The fruits of the inner man begin only with the shedding of tears. When you reach the place of tears, then know that your spirit has come out from the prison of this world and has set its foot upon the [earthly] path that leads toward the [other world]. Your spirit begins at this moment to breathe the wonderful air that's there, and it starts to shed tears."

— Kallistos Ware adapting a passage from "Mystic Treatises by Isaac of Nineveh," quoted by Ware on pp. 26–27 of The Ladder of Divine Ascent

A cautionary word. Whenever the words "gift of tears" come up in casual conservation today, there's always someone who jumps up and says, "Hey, I can do that!" Yes, there's a certain glamour surrounding the mystical gifts but, in truth, there's much that's unpleasant about them.

For example, the gift of tears wreaks havoc with one's eyes, encrusts the lids, imperils the sight, requires others to sustain you while you're enjoying this so-called spiritual gift. Eventually, as the tears gutter downward, they turn a perfectly normal face into the sad, droopy face of a bloodhound. Francis of Assisi (fifteenth century) welcomed the gift; Ignatius Loyola (sixteenth century) declined gratefully, but eventually it was thrust upon him.

When a priest from his own Society of Jesus (known as the Jesuits), inquired about the gift of tears, Ignatius felt it necessary to discern some spirits.

"Some indeed have tears naturally, when the higher motion of the soul makes itself felt in the lower, or because God our Lord, seeing that it would be good for them, allows them to melt into tears. But this doesn't mean that they have greater charity or that they are more effective than others who enjoy no tears."

Then Ignatius told the priest what he really thought.

"Even if it were in my power to give this gift to you, I wouldn't. It wouldn't help your charity, and it might even be harmful both to your head and your health; that's to say, it stands in the way of every act of charity. So don't lose heart then just because your eyes haven't turned into spigots" (*Selected Letters of St. Ignatius Loyola*, #28 To Father Nicholas Goudanus, "On the Gift of Tears," Rome, November 22, 1553).

Spiritual writers do encourage sinners to shed tears, but spiritual ones only. Some sinners do shed real tears but only during times of prayer. Some few do experience tearing that won't stop, even outside of times of prayer. If and when that occurs, the sinner should run, not walk, to the nearest spiritual director or ophthalmologist for relief. But, in the ordinary course of events, a modest box of Kleenex should cover most of one's praying needs for a lifetime. —W.G.

46

Touring the Works

Your house, Lord? It's out of this world! What else can I say?
(Psalm VUL 25:8; NRSV 26:8)

How I wish today was the day I died and Heaven swept me up! I'd have arrived at the peak by now. Ah well, a sneak peek would be out of the question, I suppose, let alone a tour of the whole works.

Nonetheless, I raise my eyes, trying to take the long view, and what do I halloo in the far distance but the holy city of Jerusalem. Still a-building in the Heavens with stones, Angels and Saints doing the hefting, lionizing lauds and joyful *jubilos* rising to God without end (VUL Apocalypse 21:2, 10; NRSV Revelation 21:2, 10).

Put wings on your desires, my dreary Soul, and fly away from the visible structures of the world to the invisible buildings of the Lord (Ephesians 2:22), to the new Jerusalem, the Heavenly City. Do say with the Psalmist, "Glorious things are said about you, Holy City of God." (Psalm VUL 86:3; NRSV 87:3).

ONCE ON THE PREMISES, dear Soul, imagine something you'd like to have, or so they say, and it's yours. You'd want to see God, of course. Face to face would be nice, but a glimpse through a half-opened door would do.

In one room, a conference room, seated at a round table, three stout, imposing figures. Father, Son, Spirit — the Trinity they'd have to be. I can't hear what they're saying. Opinionated, yes. Table-thumping, yes. Coming to blows, not quite yet.

Two of them I seem to know, but the third? He's a complete stranger to me, and yet I have the strange feeling we've met before.

THE LOBBIES AND BALCONIES are filled with the sweet hum of praise and adoration so typical of the citizens of this glorious town. Everywhere Celestial Celebrities loitering, swapping stories, signing autographs.

There's the Father, speaking comfortably to a crowd of them, not through proverbs whose literal meaning had led many of them on a merry chase. Just the Father, talking to them one on one about the Great Mysteries, but without all the mystery that used to accompany such discussion on earth.

There's the Beloved Friend, theirs and mine. The Word of Words. The Word in Principle. Teaching, explaining everything, filling in all the holes, no detail too small to be discussed.

TIME TO GO.

Heaven!

No longer just a brief personal memory of something that's yet to come, but the real thing!

My soul just gazes at the grand party going on.

So much to see! Couldn't find a thing out of place to save my life!

A holy place, the place of the Lord.

So this is where my Beloved Friend hangs out!

THANKS FOR GIVING US the run of Your House, Lord, if only for a tour! So much to see! So many chairs to try out! So many menus to choose from. I look forward to the day when I move into my small quarters. Until then, in good times but especially in bad times, I'll look forward to the time when I'll be a full-time resident in Your house.

THE DESIRE TO MOVE into my heavenly home is so strong, and yet I'll just have to wait my turn. But I grow stale with the waiting. Patience is my only option, and that's pathetic. I wouldn't hesitate to grumble if I thought it'd do any good.

THE SAINTS OF THE CHURCH managed to carry it off, though. They held up rather well under the assaults of the world. That's because their hearts were in Heaven.

But, Lord, if You want to extend my life, send me to the far corners of the earth. I'm prepared to make the trudge. But while I'm on the road, do please give me something to occupy my mind. More word pictures of Your Mansion would help.

47

Crashing the Party

In my Father's house there are many parties.

(John 2:4)

Here I am, dear Reader, in Heaven again, swanning about in the splendors of the Saints in the presence of God.

People I want to meet everywhere — everywhere somebody I already know!

Mary, mother of Jesus, perpetual virgin, ornament to the Curious Celestial Curia, sprigged with roses and lilies of the valley.

Patriarchs and Prophets; once they predicted the coming of Christ; now the jolly old gents feel quite satisfied with themselves in having done so.

Apostles and Disciples of the Lord; once the heralds of Christ, now crowing about Him to His very face.

A venerable, rather hairy figure — has to be the Baptist John!

The kindly old key man himself, Peter.

Paul, Doctor Egregious!

John the Evangelist, handsome in a portrait-painting sort of way, family friend, caretaker of the Virgin Mother, theologian of the Trinity Most High, one of the cornerstones of the Primitive Church, rector and founder of the Church in Asia.

Andrew, holily remembered for his upside-down cross.

James, Thomas, Philip; early lads on Jesus's list, giving first legs to the early Church

Apostles and Evangelists everywhere, all columns of the early Church.

Martyrs galore, soldiers of Christ, purpled by their own blood, scarred by their own fidelity.

Confessors, happily remembered, not for their purple blood — they died in bed — but for their purple prose condemning life in the secular world.

Doctors of the Church, learned gents, whose writings drew a vivid image of sanctity and gave solid support to the arguments of the early Church.

Virgins, young and old, praising the Lord in harmony; always grateful, always upbeat, always alert in their contemplation of God.

THE JOY OF THE SAINTS! If only one could snatch a bit of it! That would make the great pilgrimage much less of a trudge!

Alas, dear Reader, where I hang out, there are only labors and dolors, frontal assaults of temptation, bereavements of the age.

48

Paying
One's Respects

King and God both — no doubt about it!

(Psalm VUL 43:5; NRSV 44:4)

Still another tour, still another guide.

So what are you waiting for, dear Soul? Get off your duff! Come. Enter the place where the admirable tabernacle is, and proceed to the penthouse of God, as the Psalmist described it (VUL 41:5; NRSV 42:4).

It's the decent sort of thing to do now. The ones ahead of you in the file are finishing their tour of the works. All that's left is to stop by and pay their respects to Our Lord Jesus Christ. Yes, the Savior and Redeemer. Head of every principate and potentate. Joy and crown of all the Saints. Firm hope and certain expectation of all the Faithful.

He's the one who made you and redeemed you. He labored for you, fought and conquered for you. He lawyers for you, puts your sins in the best possible light, tries to explain them away, as John said in his First (2:1–2). He's consoler, provider, promoter, governor. He's unique, singular, one of a kind. And what's more? He's yours. He grazes among the lilies, as the

Canticle puts it, and lingers between your breasts (VUL 2;16; NRSV Song of Solomon 2:16).

So, who could ask for anyone more? Who else has loved you with such Charity?

Yes, approach Him. Present yourself to Him. Open your heart to Him. Unlock the baggage of your Soul and let Him search the damp contents.

DEAR SOUL, there's no better teacher for you. When it comes to revealing what importance hope and counsel have in the course of human affairs, and yet what variance they have in so many different events, He's the one.

When you're with Him, tell Him about yourself. Don't worry. Whatever you tell Him, He'll hold in deepest confidence (VUL Tobias 4:20; NRSV Tobit 4:19).

Human hope is hapless, according to Jesus son of Sirach (34:1). Divine hope, on the other hand, is boundless.

Through Him you'll have access to the Father. From Him every grace will be given to you. And further investments in your virtue will be made from time to time.

So sad or glad, you'll always get a warm welcome from Him.

He's been called many things over the course of time. Mirror of Life. Norm of Justice. Light Ever Burning in the Soul. Lover of Virtue. Joy of Conscience.

Now that You've met Him in person once, you'll be able to think about all the other delectable names He's been called. Because of Him the bitters and the contraries will become the tolerables. And once tolerated, they'll be pleasing to His love.

In a nutshell, as Paul wrote to the Romans, all creatures and created things come from Him, and through Him and in Him are all things (11:36).

To Him principally every intention, every action, every conversation, every reading, prayer, meditation speculation refer back to Him.

Through Him salvation is given to you, and eternal life prepared for you.

Because of Him you won't have to magnify death or belittle life. Just put your faith in His fidelity — that's the least you should do. And for His Honor and Love you offer to do anything.

So that's the tour guide's introduction. Now feel free to enter — don't just stand there — and give thanks to your Redeemer.

At last, sweetest Jesus, it's You!

I should've brought a housewarming gift, but I didn't know what. I could've shopped for something appropriate but, I thought, wouldn't You have it already? So isn't a payola like that almost a moot question? I'd give You my purse, but there's never anything in it. So there's nothing really I can give You. But that can't be right.

The only things of value I have are Humbleness, Poorness, Nothingness — tattered possessions all.

After all You're the one who's supposed to have written, "Whatever you give to Me...."

The choruses of Angels who are always entertaining You — some of them will speak on my behalf.

All I want to do is join the Celestial Choir, intoning *jubilo* after *jubilo*.

Up to this point, in honor of Your Holy Name, I should've done much, and yet I've hardly been able to lift my little finger! The least I could've done was read about You, write about You, sing about You, work for You, suffer for You. I should've exulted You, praised You, magnified You, glorified You. But, now that I'm right here in front of You, I'll pay my respects to You in a dignified way. You're my God, the one whom I've always believed in, loved, sought, yearned for.

Do SOMETHING, ANYTHING, the Psalmist cried out, that'll allow me to see Your one-of-a-kind countenance (VUL 85:17; NRSV 86:16).

IN MY MIND'S EYE I prostrate myself at Your feet because You thought it worth Your while to prostrate Yourself on the cross for me.

Write my name in the Book of Life, Lord. Blot it but don't smudge it. A question. Once written, can my name be deleted? Oops! Did I offend You with my request? Are You going to be mad at me again?

THE MATHEMATICS OF MERITS

Quantifying the redemption, breaking it down into its simplest unit, the merit, may sound silly, but is it really? The first Christians didn't think so. For them the vital operational drive in all human activity was that each good work or act done in this world earned one or more merits. The end result of such a lifetime of activity was of great consequence. Enough merits equal Heaven. Not enough, Hell.

Put another way, a merit is a unit of or share in the salvational or redemptive fund equal to the output of one good act done in time but redeemable at a later date.

Yes, the metaphor of international investment banking seems appropriate here.

Consider this passage from the beginning of the next chapter, "Asking for a Loan." The Soul is speaking to the Lord. The thought is Kempis's; the metaphor, mine.

"I'm an unhappy bloke, I want to do right, but I just can't seem to do it. The Saints committed many meritorious acts during their lifetimes and hence built up a lot of afterlife credits. But I just can't get going. I'm nothing like a saint. Yet I have the nerve, right in front of You, in Your very own presence, to ask the impossible. To give me, from Your Heavenly Treasury, enough credit to enter Your Heavenly Kingdom by the front door" (*Consolations*, 49).

Needless to say, this isn't a theological explanation of the redemptive act. It's merely a metaphorical one trying to explain Kempis's understanding in the fifteenth century. In the sixteenth century, the century after his death, all these notions would undergo further refinements by both Catholics and Protestants. —W.G.

49

Asking for a Loan

Christ lends a certain amount of grace to each person.
(Ephesians 4:7)

I'm an unhappy bloke, I want to do right, but I just can't seem to do it. The Saints comitted many meritorious acts during their lifetimes and hence built up a lot of afterlife credits. But I just can't get going. I'm nothing like a saint. Yet I have the nerve, right in front of You, Lord, in Your very own presence, to ask the impossible. To give me, from Your Heavenly Treasury, enough credit to enter Your Heavenly Kingdom by the front door.

Failing that, I'd like to ask You to look under the carpet for a credit or two — just enough to enter the Heavenly Kingdom by the rear door.

I KNOW, I KNOW, I truly know, Lord, that this rambling conversation is about the next life. That's why I have the nerve to ask for a loan. Considering how much Your Precious Blood paid for me, I know You have the resources. With this request, I'm going for broke even though I don't have a hope in the world of getting the loan.

JUST LOOK AT my scantiness and neediness, most clement Jesus. Pay attention to the affection of my heart, which I direct to and have only for You. Not because I'm worthy but because you're worthy. Unworthy that I am, yet you didn't think it unworthy of Yourself to touch me with a healing hand.

My Impurity frightens me. But Your great Piety and Humility draw me again and again, and lead me to You.

You became man, yes, but You also consented, in what must have been a moment of madness, to suffer death and burial for Man the Sinner.

And so is it any wonder that I flee to You? Over and over I've looked for good in myself and yet each time I came up empty-handed.

Fill me, flog me, my spiritual strength is flagging.

You made me desire You, it wasn't my idea first, but that's why I'm right here in front of You today. You're my hope, implored the Psalmist; my ticket to the land of the living (VUL 141:6; NRSV 14:5).

My soul's desire is to be with You in the Kingdom of Heaven. My time hasn't come yet, but I want You to know, Lord, I'll wait for You as long as it takes; that's to say, all the way to the last day, to the last hour at end of the world. In the meantime, Your name will always be on my lips. I won't forget all Your Charity on my behalf. I'll keep You present in my life by Faith and Sacrament.

I DON'T THINK I could go on living this life if I didn't have this hope in You, O Lord. I'd dance for joy in this world, but I'd fear that I'd remain without consolation and joy. Hence, I've decided to place my joy in You.

Often I've wandered off, too often really, and too often I've had wishy-washy, slipsliding thoughts. Instead I should've held You firmly in my memory and imagination.

Because I don't have the strength to delve Your divinity or grasp Your truth, it's safer for me in this present state to turn to Your Holy Humanity. That's to say, when I'm in touch with Your humanity, I'm not all that far from Your divinity.

THANK YOU, Jesus good and sweet, for thinking it worth Your while to become my brother, my mouth, my flesh!

Thanks also to Your Holy Mother Mary, who thought it worth her while to say yes to Your Father's incredible proposition.

TELLING THE BEADS

Prayer beads arose in the East, and it wouldn't be surprising to learn that the Magi, when they made their fabled visit to the baby Jesus, left behind some lovely examples of the prayer bead art.

Essentially, beads are an abacus, a counting device when one feels compelled to say a prayer not just once, but a number of times in joyful or tearful succession. In just such a way the early Christians used fingers, pebbles, knotted cords, strings of beads or berries.

In the fourth century the Egyptian Abbot Paul, when he wanted to say the same prayer three hundred times, put three hundred pebbles into his lap, then dropped them one by one as he said them one by one.

Archeological records have revealed fragments of prayer beads in the tomb of the holy abbess Gertrude of Nivelles who lived in the seventh century; more prayer bead fragments were found in the tombs of St. Norbert and of St. Rosalia of the twelfth century.

In the eighth century the *Penitentials,* or rule books pertaining to penitents, prescribed the Pater Noster (Our Father) as an appropriate penance in clusters of twenty, fifty, one hundred. The strings of beads, with the aid of which such penances were ticked off, gradually came to be known as Paternosters.

In the course of the eleventh, twelfth, and thirteenth centuries, Paternosters came into extensive use, especially in the religious orders. At certain times corresponding to the canonical hours, lay brothers and lay sisters were obliged to say a certain number of Our Fathers as an equivalent of the clerical obligation of reading the Divine Office. Likewise the military orders, notably the Knights of St. John, adopted the Paternoster beads as a part of the equipment of lay members.

In the fifteenth century, swagging the beads at one's belt was a distinctive sign of membership in a religious confraternity or third order.

As it will in all things spiritual, Fashion eventually reared her lovely head. Muscular monks and friars began to sport beads made from coral, crystal, and amber. Plump nuns tarted themselves up by wearing their decorative beads as necklaces. To prohibit such displays of flesh and flash, unappreciative superiors did what they could.

Always there were those who wore the Paternosters and Avemarias (Hail Marys) as signs of penance. Bands of pilgrims especially displayed them openly when visiting the Christian shrines, churches, and holy places.

Prayer beads came to be appraised as valuable objects of jewelry and apprized as appropriate gifts between parties in a spiritual friendship.

If the beads had been worn or fingered by a person revered for sanctity, they automatically acquired value as collectibles.

Even if they'd merely touched the relics or grazed the reliquary of a saint, they were piously believed to have acquired something of the patina, the charisma, of that saintly individual when he or she was alive.

But, mostly, beads just made the business of repetitionary prayer more efficient. —W.G.

50

Hailing Mary

Here she comes, the Queen, in designer gown, cloth of gold,
imported from Ophir, with lovely rainbow trim!

(Psalm VUL 44:10; NRSV 45:9)

Yes, Lord Jesus, I'm a cipher when it comes to merit — I'm continually flogged by my *flagrante delicto's;* nevertheless my faith in Your Passion remains steadfast. As does my passion for Your holy mother, Mary. She's the subject of my meditation today. Surely You've no objection. Angels do it all the time. Why not we humans some of the time?

"WHO'S THAT WOMAN coming up from the desert, airs of Paradise trailing behind her, her head on her beloved's shoulder?" (VUL Canticle of Canticles 8:5; NRSV Song of Solomon 8:5).

Holy Mary, Lovely Lady, it never occurred to me that your glory and honor, your pulchritude and magnitude, might be the subject of my humble meditation. That's because I'm earth and ash, actually worse than that. I'm a sinner and a sucker for all kinds of evil stuff.

You, however, have been made higher than Heaven. You have the world under your feet. You're lit with honor and reverence. Your piety is said to be beyond words, beyond thoughts. So why am I so drawn to you? Probably because you're so drawn to me. Your reputation as comfort to the Desolate and pleasure to the Wretched is well known.

WHAT'S WRONG WITH ME? What's missing from my life? Well, all consolations and comforts, which are, of course, Graces from your Son. Which is another way of saying that, without His help, I'm totally helpless.

You, however, Lovely Lady, if you think it worth your while to pay some attention to my spiritual poverty, you can come to my aid in many ways. Chiefly by rekindling my fires, refiring my ovens; that's to say, by adding another poor soul to your never failing breast. Whenever I've been bested, busted, by some worldly pressure, I run back to you without a fear in my heart. That's because your nursing knows no bounds.

May I, Lovely Lady, give way to some small speculation about your *Gloria in Excelsis*. Protocol requires I greet you with the pompous honorifics due a personage of your stature. But I want to take a little time to add a little warmth to my greeting, a dash of hope. That having been said, I approach you reverently, devoutly, and confidently.

Now, Lovely Lady, don't expect too much from me. I'm no Gabriel. Don't expect the extravagant greeting he gave you some centuries ago, with head reverentially inclined and hands affectionately expanded — a greeting ceaselessly repeated and imitated by Angels and other Celestial Spirits. With all this in memory, I approach you as humbly as I can. Beyond that, I don't have a clue as what to say or do.

LOVELY LADY, just as you love to hear your Son's Holy Name, so do we like to hear yours.

One thing is sure. When I say your name, things happen.

Ave Maria, Hail Mary!
Heaven rejoices!
Ave Maria, Hail Mary!
Satan regurgitates!
Ave Maria, Hail Mary!
This world shrinks from comparison.
Ave Maria, Hail Mary!
Out goes sadness, in comes Joy.
Ave Maria, Hail Mary!
Sloth slinks off.
Ave Maria, Hail Mary!
My heart grows damp!
Ave Maria, Hail Mary!
Devotion increases.
Ave Maria, Hail Mary!
Compunction revives.
Ave Maria, Hail Mary!
Hope succeeds.
Ave Maria, Hail Mary!
Consolation increases.
Ave Maria, Hail Mary!
My soul feels new life.
Ave Maria, Hail Mary!
Affection herself is comforted.

AVE MARIA, Holy Mary!

Yes, the sweetness of this angelic greeting can be appreciated in some small way here on earth, but it's full meaning is known only to the Sender. Even Gabriel had only a clue.

But I, Lovely Lady, when I say *Ave Maria, gratia plena* (Hail Mary, full of grace), I bend my voice in humility.

Therefore, Lovely Lady, please accept my humble greeting. And please know, when you respond, you raise my heart a step higher.

Up to this point in my life, I've merited only wrath for my sins, and this has made your Son sad, gloomy, morose. But if I set out to say an Ave Maria for each and every sin I've ever committed, then I begin to feel an incredible lightening of being. Would that all Blessed Spirits and Souls of the Just might say just one Ave Maria for my universal excesses and negligences, for all my vain, unclean, perverse thoughts! And may all the Ave Marias — mine as well as theirs — rise like wisps from the thurible.

But now, every time I say *Ave Maria,* I feel like the Archangel Gabriel himself stealing into your private places and saluting you with private honorifics; now not so private in the first chapter of the Gospel of Luke.

I wish the whole world could join me as I mouth each and every word.

Ave Maria, gratia plena, Dominus tecum (Hail Mary, full of grace, the Lord is with you, Luke 1:28).

Benedicta tu in mulieribus (Blessed are you among women, Luke 1:28, 48).

Benedictus fructus ventris tui (Blessed is the fruit of your womb, Luke 1:28, 42). Amen.

This is the Angelic Salutation. This is the prayer. Short on words but long in mysteries. Like pebbles into a pond, ripples to ponder. Sweet like honey, precious like gold. Said from the mouth, echoing in the heart. Repeated by lips more pure than mine. Woe to those who say the Hail Mary so often without attention or reverence!

From this moment on I'll be more devout, fervent, when I say the Hail Mary. Wherever I am. Whether together in chorus in the chapel or alone in my cell, either in the garden or at the gate, wherever I'll be in the future.

AND NOW, LOVELY LADY, after these lovely words, what do I seek? The grace of God. Would that you'd intervene and give weight to my petition! Yes, something of the grace that, with the Angel Gabriel as witness, and in God's presence, you received from the Plenitude of Grace, Grace Galore!

No PETITION IS DEARER than the grace and mercy of God. If I have them, asked Paul in his First to the Corinthians, what else do I need (12:9)? There's no sense in asking for anything else. With it I can do everything. Without it, I can't lift a finger.

I have all sorts of sickness of soul. The only medicine that works is Divine Grace.

There's another thing. I have such a lack of spiritual wisdom and knowledge. But Divine Grace is the Greatest Teacher and Doctor of Celestial Discipline.

Grace dissuades me from seeking something I don't need or wishing to know something I shouldn't know. It also advises me and teaches me to humble myself, to restrain myself.

This is the Grace you could ask for me, Lovely Lady.

PRAYING THE BEADS

Mary was just a humble Jewish miss before the Archangel came a-knocking. No, she'd never say no, she thought to herself even before the Archangel had finished his fine and polished presentation, but, yes, God had to ask. With that her life took a dramatic turn.

That moment in human and divine history has become memorialized in the Ave Maria (Hail Mary), sometimes called the Angelic Salutation; after the Pater Noster (Our Father), it's the second most popular prayer in Christian history. It has three parts.

First presents the words used by the Angel Gabriel in saluting the Blessed Virgin (Luke 1:28): "Hail Mary full of grace, the Lord is with you, blessed are you among women."

Second borrows Elizabeth's words of greeting (Luke 1:42): "and blessed is the fruit of your womb (Jesus)."

Third includes a petition, which was added some centuries later: "Holy Mary, Mother of God, pray for us sinners now and at the hour of our death. Amen."

In the first Christian millennium, saying Hail Marys grew in popularity until the clergy had to program them into a proper devotional channel, with the counting being done on circlets of beads. The circlet itself was called a *rosarium* (Rosary); each bead an *Ave*; each *Ave*, a rose.

The Hail Mary itself appears in decades or groups of ten. Ten times in each decade. Each decade is preceded by an Our Father and followed by a Glory be to the Father. And there are brief opening and closing prayers.

The essence of the Rosary is the rhythmic repetition of a friendly prayer to an attentive mother. But repetition, no matter how comfy, how homely, will soon send the voice wandering in one direction and the mind in another. To counter this, the clergy proposed to put the mind to work meditating on a scene, any scene, from the lives of Jesus and Mary. Hundreds of mysteries, as these scenes were called, suggested themselves.

Eventually, for public recitation, there emerged three groups of five decades each: the Joyful, Sorrowful, and Glorious Mysteries; and a Rosary was then said to consist of fifteen decades. For private recitation, of course, the prayerful soul could pick and choose and say as many as it wanted.

This solution may sound schizoid and in a way it is, but we moderns have learned to deal with it. Nowadays cable news networks routinely run five or six items simultaneously on one screen. Needless to say, if one is at all drawn to the Rosary as a prayer, then he or she can adapt rather easily to the comfortable repetition and the prayerful meditation.

Yes, the Rosary is a repetitionary prayer. Trouble is, for some, by virtue of the wording of its chief prayer, the Hail Mary, it's also a petitionary prayer. All prayers should be addressed to God alone, but here this one comes along addressed to someone rather less than God. And what about the Saints?

Catholic theologians centuries ago addressed this problem by distinguishing three levels of worship. *Latria,* or adoration suitable only for God. *Hyperdulia,* or high veneration appropriate only for Mary. *Dulia,* or low veneration properly given to Angels and Saints. Yet, for all the distinctions, in the minds and souls of some, the appearance of idolatry persists, especially when the wording of all three modes of worship appears substantially the same.

In *Letters to Malcolm* (1964) C. S. Lewis addressed this issue. As a Protestant he decided that he couldn't pray *to* the Saints (Mary included) as the Romans did but that he could pray *with* the Saints (Mary included) as the Angels did.

As chapters 50–52 of *Consolations* indicate, Kempis could write knowingly and admiringly of Mary, Mother of Jesus and Queen of Heaven, without at the same time stepping on any toes, human or divine.

In Kempis's own time, the Rosary was at the height of its popularity in Europe. As an instance, Florentine painter Bastiano Mainardi (1460–1513) did a work entitled *The Rosary.* Two facing panels. On one there are men, and on the other, women, all standing as they prayed the Rosary. Each panel containing at least twenty people. It's a Who's Who of medieval life, both spiritual and secular, from clergy and royalty down to ordinary folk and children; alas, no greyhounds. The artist's theme? Everyone prayed the Rosary. That's to say, everyone who was anyone in the Middle Ages prayed the Rosary. —W.G.

51

Having a Word with Mary

If I read your lips aright, you just paid me a compliment.

(Psalm VUL 44:3; NRSV 45:2)

"Holy Mary, Lady Mary, may I have a word?"

"Oh dear me, no, not me. It's my Son you want to talk to. He's blessed us all with every spiritual grace."

"No, dearest Mother, it's you I want to talk to."

"Well, look at me, a sweet mess, and no one to talk to."

"That's not true."

"Isn't it? Well, here I sit on oodles of Charity and boodles of Sweetness. I could give them all away if I wanted to, but no one comes to call." (Sirach 24:26)

"That's just not true, dear Lady. I've come."

"And a sad mess you are!"

"Yes, I'm a sinner."

"Well, one sinner is nice, but where are the rest of you?"

"Don't be sad, dear Lady, they're coming."

"No, they're not."

"Yes, they are."

"No, they're not."

"You seem to forget that you're the ladder Sinners climb. You're the hope and forgiveness of Defendants in the Divine

Dock. You're the consolation of the terminally Sad. You're the special Joy of the Saints."

"Well, dear Soul, I don't know all about that."

"Admit it, dear Lady."

"Well, over time I do seem a source of amusement to many."

"And indeed of immense help. So why do you keep it a secret?"

"I don't have a secret exactly. It's just not appropriate for a woman of my position to crow out loud at bequests granted, requests furthered, and so on."

"Well, what's your real secret?"

"Jesus is my secret, and my joy. Yes, He's my Son, and yes, I've nursed Him and nurtured Him and continue to do so; not only Him, but also His friends, and indeed anyone else who asks."

"What's behind all this mothering?"

"Love me, love My son, and vice versa."

"Any of His friends, you say?

"Yes."

"Really, that many. What advice would you have for the near-friends and would-be friends?"

"Well, don't wonder whether you're one of the sinless ones or the sinful ones; just tell me what the case against you is. Then, when your case, each case, comes to the Father and then to the Son, I'll represent you."

"And what would be your expectation?"

"I'd fully expect that the case would be dismissed and your slate wiped clean through the Holy Spirit."

"And just how would you expect to be reimbursed, dear Lady?

"Oh, don't worry your soul about that. It's prepaid, you know."

"What an inviting proposition!"

"It's not a proposition. It's an invitation, and I'd very much appreciate it if you'd pass the word on to your friends, and they to their friends, and so on."

"A better invitation I've never had, Lovely Lady, but we sinners tend to think that they're only lovely words. That's to say, if all of us showed up at your doorstep, you'd just tell us to shove off."

"No, really, I mean it. I expect all of you to come."

"But suppose, just suppose, we all do come, but just for the refreshments, and with no intention of asking for help, for an oodle or a boodle?"

"Are you a sinner?"

"Yes, I am."

"Am I looking down my nose at you?"

"No, you're not."

"Am I pinching my nose as you approach?"

"No, you're not."

"Then yes, I mean everyone to come."

"But suppose only one of us came forward penitent?"

"I'd rejoice with the Angels of God in Heaven and toss the glitter of Charity in the air. That's because the Precious Blood of my Son still pumps and indeed still covers the world."

"What's your specific message, Lovely Lady?"

"So, what are you waiting for, my children? Do approach me. Come close, closer, closer still. Just watch my zeal as I approach, on your behalf, God, my Son, Jesus Christ."

"But won't your Son be angry at all the sins we've committed?"

"Sometimes the fit comes upon Him, but I know how to relieve Him of His wrath."

"How's that?"

"I placate Him with the prayers I taught Him. And after that you'd never recognize Him as the person you offended. Glad smiles, glad hands!"

"This is a pretty picture you paint, Lovely Lady, but by and large sinners are a sluggish lot. Surely you have a word for them."

"Tell them that they don't have to tell their sins to me. Sinners! They're so reticent at first, but once they get going, they want to tell you every itsy-bitsy detail of every single sin they've ever committed. Just tell me you're a sinner, and I'll negotiate the rest."

BEFRIENDING MARY

Jesus wasn't the only person to come to Kempis's room-within-a-room. Apparently, Mary was a frequent visitor too. At least according to Kempis himself in one of his sermons.

"Brothers, in the likely event that the Malignant Enemy wrests your attention away from praising God and Mary, don't downsize your prayer schedule. If anything, hot up your Marian prayer. Some suggestions of how to do just that.

"Salute Mary. Think Mary. Name Mary. Honor Mary. Glorify Mary. Bow to Mary. Just commend yourself to Mary.

"Meet with Mary. Enjoy silence with Mary. Rejoice with Mary. Sorrow with Mary. Labor with Mary. Pray with Mary. Walk with Mary. Just sit with Mary.

"With Mary look for Jesus. With Mary carry Jesus on your hip. With Mary and Jesus live in Nazareth. With Mary go to Jerusalem. With Mary stand at the cross of Jesus. With Mary mourn Jesus. With Mary bury Jesus. With Mary and Jesus rise. With Mary and Jesus ascend. With Mary and Jesus live and die.

"Brothers, if you think these things over and put them into practice, the Devil will be totally flummoxed, and you'll make progress in the spiritual life. And Jesus will listen to His mother with special deference as she readies her next list of requests."

> — Excerpt from "De veneratione et commemoratione Beatae Mariae Virginis" (On the Veneration and Commemoration of the Blessed Virgin Mary), Sermon XXI, as it appears in *Sermones ad Novicios Regulares* (Sermons to the Novices on the Monastic Track), *Omnia Opera* (1905), 6:204–205.

—W.G.

52

Mothering a Sinner

Among those standing around the cross
was His mother Mary.

(John 19:25)

"Don't stand with your backs to me," said the Lovely Lady. "Turn round and come to me. No need to tell me your sins; spare me the details."

"You make it sound so easy," said the Soul.

"And they should do it now. They shouldn't waste time. Don't abuse God's mercy and my clemency. Avoid every offense."

"Why?" asked the Soul. "There's a lovely leisure in your presence."

"You don't know, do you, the moment when God will turn from you, totally indifferent to you and your case."

"No, I don't."

"Mark what I say here, dear Soul. I'm a weeper, chief weeper for wretched people everywhere. And of all the faithful, I'm the most pious advocator."

"Your words, Lovely Lady, soothe my troubled Soul, smooth my ruffled feathers in a heavenly sweetness sort of way. Yes, I'll pass the word along again. You bring smiles to the Sad and tears to the Glad."

"Just so, dear Soul."

"Before you spoke, Lovely Lady, I felt bad, but now I feel better. Now if I understand you aright, Lovely Lady, you're my advocate in your Son's court, knowing as you do all the details of my case. I commend myself to His mercy from this hour on."

"What's the trouble, dear child? Who are they, the ones who want to harm you?"

"Everyone," replied the Soul. "I'm afraid. I'm a bundle of nerves."

"I'll look into it, child of mine. I live, and my Son lives, my Jesus, your brother, who's at an advantageous position near the Father. He's a Faithful Pontiff and Intercessor on behalf of the damage caused by your sins. In Him you can put your best hope. He's the Giver of Life and the Destroyer of Death.

"The Father sired Him in eternity," the Lovely Lady went on. I mothered Him in this world. Through me He was given to the whole world as part of the salvational process."

"O happy hour, O pious Virgin Mary, when you thought it worth your while to approach my fibrillating heart. It takes only a few of your words — touching, haunting — to rouse me, get me going again, make me feel that I still have a chance."

I FEEL a prayer coming on.

Blessed Mother Mary, nursing your Son with the sweet milk of consolation and mothering us with the sweet grace of salvation! No wonder you can't refuse your beloved Son, and no wonder you can't say no to the person who's knocking your door down.

O Virgin of Virgins, Queen of the World, Lady of the Angels, lead the way, and draw me after you!

"I'm MARY, the mother of Jesus. Jesus who? Jesus Christ, son of the Living God. He's the savior of the world, the King of Heaven and Earth; Lord of the Angels and Redeemer of the Faithful, Judge of the Living and the Dead. He's the hope of the Pious, the consolation of the Devout, the peace of the Meek, the wealth of the Poor, the glory of the Humble, the fortitude of the Debilitated, the way for the Lost, the light of the Blind. The crutch for the Limp. The unction of the Arid. The lifting up of the Oppressed. The first aid to the Troubled, the refuge of all the brood."

53

Bending under the Burden

At the name of the Lord every knee should bend!
(Psalm VUL 71:17; NRSV 72:17)

I don't want this little book to end, dear Lord, before I say
one important thing! That is, I serve You and You only in
whatever I do — reading, writing, speaking, thinking.

You're the beginning point of my every work, and the ending point. What You give me, You get back from me. Tides
in, tides out. That's to say, I do what You tell me. I give all to
You and retain nothing for myself. This I do, not out of fear.
Far from it. When I do my accounting for You, it returns
nothing but joy.

Yes, dear Lord, I talk a good game, but much of the time I
don't deliver. I'm just a slug, so what can I possibly give back to
You? If I do what You've ordered me to do, I don't count that
as service, or even servitude. As for my being a slug, well, we
both know how that happened. You've whittled me down to a
pile of wood curls, as the Psalmist wrote, humbled me down
to the simplest truth; that's to say, to You (VUL 118:71; NRSV
119:71). Odd thing happened, though, but nice nevertheless.
The less I became, the more You became. The more matter I
shed, the purer my praise became.

Truth to tell, dear Lord, don't stop! Keep the pressure on. I just want to praise You with heart and voice. Without You, the best I can manage is a few pathetic peeps, which no one wants to hear, least of all myself. You're forever in my heart! You're forever in my canticles.

Praising You, dear Lord, leads to the broad highway (Jeremiah 17:14). Not praising You when one has the chance leads only up a cul-de-sac (Psalm VUL 70:6; NRSV 71:6).

If I may get soupy for a moment, dear Lord, and I know how squiffy that makes You feel, but nonetheless. The person who gets just a little, a sip or a whiff, of Your Heavenly Delights, quickly finds that he's lost his taste for all earthly delights, no matter how sticky, how sweet.

One scintilla will do it. Just strike one spark of Charity, and it'll soon turn into a bonfire, incarnating, even incinerating, everything around it, leaving behind only a few wisps for me to remember You by.

ANOTHER THING I want to record for the record.

Following You, pursuing You, chasing after You — all exercises in Love, I know. How exhausting and yet how exhilarating! Love is a burden but, strangely, Love is also a beast of burden. So who can complain? Well, I've complained, often every step of the way, which is a sure sign that I had comparatively little love in my own pockets. Best thing to do, maybe, is just to empty my pockets. Only then will I find that these few pathetic objects have been mightily revalued as tokens of Love.

54

Meditating on Love

Thinking about love is thinking about God.
(1 John 4:8)

Some thoughts about love.

LOVE DOESN'T RESPECT my own personal convenience. Which is another way of saying, it doesn't shrink from inconveniencing me from time to time. The only approval it needs is Yours.

YOUR LOVE, LORD? How sweet it smells! How good it sounds! How fine it looks! How soft it feels!

WOULD THAT it'd oblige me to Your service forever!

WOULD THAT it'd sweep me up and spirit me away and make me one of Your own! Freeman and captive! Privately and personally Yours in each and every respect. Your slave — that's what I am, Lord. Yours, I say, because you bought me on the block.

YES, I'M FREELY YOURS, and I don't feel the least embarrassment about it. I've never had a second thought about it. Give me Your hand, and I can leave everything behind.

Blow on the spark, urge it onward and upward until it envelops my heart. The result is cool, blue, beautiful flame. Not a vice or defect anywhere to be seen. Consuming every sin.

Now, dear Lord, I'm not forgetting that my service to You doesn't amount to a hill of beans. But it does help me a bit if I do something new for You every now and then.

Would that I could do something great for You and not have to be silent about it! Instead I do something pitifully small and blab about it as though it were something incredibly big.

You've given me so much to be thankful for over the years, but I've been such a thankless prat! That's when the pangs and pains punish my heart. It's just that I'm an empty vase, a cracked urn. Unable to hold a thing to satisfy a thirst.

Therefore, what should I do?

I mean, I've got to give something back. It just isn't right to appear in Your Presence and try to make a joke about it. *Oops! Sorry about that! I don't know what I was thinking. I don't know how I forgot, but wasn't I supposed to bring something for the occasion?*

I mean, I know already that every ingrate who approaches You — and I'm the supreme example of that — turns Your stomach. But I also happen to know that if I had anything to give You, no matter how crappy or creepy it might be, You'd turn it into something wonderful.

What would You like to have, Beloved Lord? You don't really want any of the sorts of things I could easily lay my hands on. So just why is it, as the Psalmist might put it, that You still want something, anything, from me (VUL 15:2;

NRSV 16:2)? A piddle? A tiddle? Whatever? No one's richer than You or poorer than I, and yet You want to snag a little something from me, of all people?

ARE YOU FINISHED? asked the Lord. Are you bloody well finished?

What do I want from you, you pathetic ingrate? I want everything! But I'll settle for something, anything. And what's more, I'll give you the Grace to do it. And by doing it you'll be returning the Grace to Me. It's as simple as that. Equal bond? Mutual Charity! Pals forever? Friends forever!

Give yourself to Me. That may sound like a lot to you, but to Me, it's a pitifully small gift, barely visible to the naked eye. But do it, and you'll find that there's nothing left to give — you've given it all.

I FEEL a prayer coming on, says my Soul.

Jesu, Font of Good, Font of Life, Font of Grace, Font of Sweetness, Font of Wisdom! Drizzle my humble but pious gift with Your Grace. Remind me of my manners always. There's nothing You like better than a thank-you note. It's the least I can do.

ONE THING THOUGH. All the sins I've committed have my name on them. None of them may be attributed to You whatsoever. All the good things I've done? Well, that's another story. I have You to thank for them. Which I really haven't done yet.

Let me just mention three of them.

Creation . . .

Redemption . . .

Justification . . .

55

Giving Thanks for Creation

May the name of the Lord be blessed forever!
(Psalm VUL 71:17; NRSV 72:17)

First Favor I give You thanks for, dear Lord, is Creation;
that's to say, everything You thought it worth Your while to
create. Especially for lording it over all the beasts and birds
of the sky. More especially for the rational world of which
I'm a part. Most especially for making us in Your own image
and likeness, with capacity enough to hold eternal wisdom
and participate in the Truth.

FOR EVERYTHING I am, live, and taste, I offer my perpetual
thanks to You. And I hope and pray all Your other creatures
will do the same.

I BLESS YOU, Father and Lord of Heaven and Earth, Who
out of nothing made everything through Your Son and in the
Holy Spirit. Not that anyone was crowding You to do it —
only that You wanted to do it. A display of power (Psalm
VUL 144:12; NRSV 145:11), yes, but a shower of mercy at the
same time.

At Your request the sky floods the plain, and the plain
brings forth crops galore. In the same easy manner, may all

Your rational creatures bless You, serve You, and carry out Your wishes.

Sun and moon can be seen and felt on the earth. At night the stars make their appropriate rounds.

Fountains gush.

Streams flow.

Fish swim.

Birds fly and sing.

Goats and deer, bucks and does prance about the mountaintops.

Sheep and cattle lie down in green pastures.

Forests are alive with footprints.

Meadows wave; fields flower; trees branch.

All are Your works, O God — all bear Your marks!

56

Giving Thanks for Redemption

He doffed His divinity and donned our humanity.

(Philippians 2:7)

Second Favor I give You thanks for, Dear Lord, is the mystery of Your Incarnation, the work of Your Redemption, the price of Your salvation. All, the fruit of Your Passion and Death. All, the work of Piety, Charity, Humility, Patience!

THIS — Humankind did nothing to merit this! This, no Angel could have done This, the Prophets just shook their heads about and wondered at. This, the Apostles shrugged at but taught. This, the Faithful, one and all, took up. This, the Elect love and cherish.

THESE GOOD DEEDS, when one stops to think about it, excite desires, inflame hearts, feed devotion; illumine the mind, purge affections; attract one toward Heaven, withdraw one from the world — all lead to Christ, and unite the Soul to Christ.

This gift dwarfs Creation, the previous gift. And the Person who made and gave both gifts is Our Lord Jesus Christ, God. For nothing born into the world would've had any value if it hadn't been redeemed by the precious gift of Your blood.

GRACE WAS SLIPPED TO ME, as well as to the Psalmist, in small packets, finally bursting into Divine Mercy (VUL 129:7; NRSV 130:7). Yes. But what accounts for the extravagant increase in Grace was the Redemption, the celestial banking institution that, apparently, has assets for initiatives like this. Without such aid from the Creator, our wounded and blasted nature couldn't have been mended.

O Father of Mercies and God of All Consolation, as Paul addressed You at the beginning of his Second to the Corinthians (1:3), to buy back Your condemned servant, You handed over Your son. O that you should do a thing like this for us! To explain it away, neither human mind nor angelic reason has any resources.

O SWEETEST JESUS, Prince and Principle of Our Salvation and End! You and You Alone could confer help on the Wretched and Condemned. For in the most humble and abject form of a slave You thought it worth Your while to walk among Humankind. With us creepy-crawlies, but without a second thought, You undertook the sentence of our dire death, with no other intention than charity toward the Distressed and Depressed.

JESU, Font of Goodness and Piety; Light of Lights; Mirror of Mirrors (VUL Book of Wisdom 7:26; NRSV Wisdom of Solomon 7:6); Majesty of God!

BY VIRTUE OF MY MEDITATION on this favor, Redemption, may my heart ascend. You wanted to show it to me and indeed to the rest of the world.

THIS SECOND FAVOR is a general one like the first, giving a boost toward salvation for everyone but not forcing the salvific end on anyone. All should choose it, but Infidelity and Malice take their toll.

For all the Elect, however, Salvation has much to recommend it. On account of Him all things were created. Through you Christ Jesus, all things were re-created.

You were made of the same stuff as we, that we might be made of the same stuff as You; that's to say, to be numbered among the children of God (VUL Book of Wisdom 5:5; NRSV Wisdom of Solomon 5:5).

Through You we have access to the Father, whose offense nobody is in a position to placate except, of course, you, about whom some words were once spoken. This is my Beloved Son in whom I'm well pleased (Matthew 17:5) — isn't He a kick in the pants?

Happy the soul who studies regularly, loves affectionately, venerates worthily, the sacraments of our redemption, and gives thanks for all.

To You, Lord, praise and honor are due. Benediction and Clarity, Thanksgiving and the Voice of Praise, Fortitude and Power, Majesty and Wisdom be to You, our Lord God, Jesus Christ, forever and forever. Amen.

57

Giving Thanks for Justification

He was handed over for our redemption,
and He rose for our justification.

(Romans 4:25)

Third Favor I give You thanks for, dear Lord, is the Grace of Justification. That's how You drew me to conversion, granting me hope of forgiveness and a plan for doing better with a view to serving You forever and ever.

This is the favor that clearly tickled the blessed Paul. He kept after his disciples lest they be unthankful for such a great favor in their own lives.

"Take a good look at your own vocations," he wrote in his First to the Corinthians, "and then you'll see that when God chose. He didn't pick the people in the know or the people in power; rather He chose the little people of the world" (1:26–27).

That description certainly fits me. I'm one of the contemptible ones, the clumsy ones in the world. I sailed away from Him, but when my ship hit the rocks, He rescued me. Since that time I've just been hanging around, picking up what I could, and serving Him here and there.

Lest I return to my old seafaring ways, I've had to cut back on my bad habits. It has nothing to do with my merits, but everything to do with Your merits, Lord. For the which I praise You extravagantly, giving me good will and relieving me of the load of sins I was dragging around.

Yes, Lord, You subjugated me, in a manner of speaking, but Your burden, such as it is, has almost no weight at all; aloeing my mind with Your Spirit, the Spirit the world knows nothing about, not a whiff, not a sip, not a smack.

GUARD MY INTENT, merciful Lord. Look down upon me and increase the gifts of Your Grace as I hang about in the lamp-light of Your world. I know the Grace of Justification isn't given to all, that it's a gift from the Father. I know also that I've done nothing to earn it — Paul again, this time from his to the Romans. If there were a pricetag, I couldn't afford it. Pure Gift — that's what it is (9:16).

If You'd wished to deal with me according to the norms of Pure Justice, Lord, You'd have sent me packing to Hell. Your piety, Your Faithfulness to the creatures You created, spared me, O Lord. And You gave me a space where I could hang out while the Son of Eternal Perdition tried to hunt me down. That's why I feel I have to return great thanks to You, Lord, for Your magnificent favor. Would that I'd responded before now to all the worthy voices in my life!

Epilogue

I beseech You, Lord, to accept this pitifully small book of mine as a token of thanks. It's also my way of serving You, repaying Your Charity in however small a way. It came from You, of course, and I return it to You as an honor. I had to finish it while I still saw Your hand in my life.

May I continue to praise You! May You continue to praise me!

If I live to be a hundred, I'll still slave for You as though it were the first hour of the first day my heart was warmed by Yours and decided to follow You.

Now, at midlife, I still trip up from time to time, but I won't despair nor will I abandon You. I'll bend the knees of my heart with much contrition and tears by offering You my bruised and battered conscience. Do mend it, make it well, by applying your grace to the site of the wound. I made a good start, and a fall every now and then won't keep me off the track for long. With Your grace I'm in this race for the long haul.

Funny thing, though, You created me out of nothing even though You knew, right from the start, that I was going to fall on my face. And not once, but many times.

With me and with the others, You forgave all our sins, the ones we committed and the ones we omitted.

You restored what had been destroyed, healed what had been bruised, brushed off the dirt, lightened up the shadows, damped down the swollen.

You rekindled the Extinct, rebuilt the Ruined, rescued the Neglected, aligned the Crooked, smoothed the Rough, restricted the Curious, herded the Wanderers, ordered the Disordered — all to change Your state of mind for the better — all that the original course of action might not lose its intensity.

As additional tokens of thanks, please accept these.

All the devout services of Holy Church.

All the unanimous consent of the whole heavenly court.

And all the Saints since the origin of the world.

All the Faithful Christians in every people and tribe and language and nation who went before us right up to this day, and who'll come after us — may they too celebrate and join choirs to sing the sweetest and most glorious name. That's the name to be eternally blessed beyond all other names.

May they say again and again, mouthing with great joy, the universal lauds worthy of saying the name of God.

All the stars in the heavens, all the fish in the sea, all the blades of grass on the earth, and last but not least, all the letters in all the books of the world.

To conclude.

In Creation You favored us with Nature. In Redemption, You gifted us with Excellence beyond which there is none. In Justification You gave us Grace.

In behalf of one and all, Sinners and Non-sinners alike, may glory be to you, Holy Trinity, Equal, One, Deity. From the beginning to now to the end. Amen.

THUS ENDS

CONSOLATIONS FOR MY SOUL.

IF I LIVE TO BE A HUNDRED

"If I live to be a hundred," Kempis wrote in his Epilogue to *Consolations,* "I'll still slave for You as though it were the first hour of the first day my heart was warmed by Yours and decided to follow You."

He got his wish, almost. A long life was indeed his, and he spent it well, praying, reading, writing. His complete works would run to seven volumes (1902–1922), filled with anthologies, chronicles, biographies, rules and regulations, sermons, maxims.

"When Death knocks, surprise him," he wrote in the *Imitation.* "Invite him in and ask what took him so long — the tea's been getting cold" (1, 23).

In chapters 15 and 16 of *Consolations,* he expressed his wishes about passing from this world to the next.

"Come, Lord Jesus, and rescue me from this alien land. Summon this pitiful servant home.... It's time that I return to You again. It's time to commend me to the earth, which is my body's true home.

"It doesn't matter how my corpse is handled or where it's finally stashed. Wherever, it won't be remote or unknown to You, my Lord and Friend....

"The thought of death doesn't upset me mightily. Your Holy Angels are known to be Your faithful assistants in this regard. As I die wearily, may they protect me virily! May they pick me up gently and leniently! May they lead me in appropriate, if humble, procession to the heavenly Paradise....

"To live for You used to mean everything; now to die for You is the only thing," Paul wrote to his Philippians

(1:21). "Much better still is to finally be at home with You in the kingdom of Heaven" (*Consolations* 16).

On August 8, 1471, then, in the ninety-second year of his age, the sixty-fifth year of his monastic life, the fifty-eighth year of his priesthood, Kempis died; dropsy was given as the cause.

He was buried in the cloister of his monastery, where he lay quietly for two centuries, even as the monastery buildings above and around his grave were being leveled by one wave of religious enthusiasm or another. The Brethren and Sistern of the Common Life, once vibrant, were no more; few records of the Brethren survived but of the Sistern virtually none.

Kempis's remains were removed to a church in Zwolle and enclosed in a reliquary. In 1688 he was made a Venerable, first step on the road to canonization; when the promoter of his cause died, however, the cause died with him. In 1897 his remains were enclosed in a monument, paid for by international subscriptions, and installed inside St. Michael's Church, Zwolle.

One scrap of his literary remains remains today that particularly sums up his life as monk, priest, and bookman extraordinaire; indeed the very incarnation of *Devotio Moderna*. It's a motto, epitaph, whatever, in Latin and Dutch.

In omnibus requiem quaesivi, sed non inveni, nisi in Hoexkens ende Boexkens.

"For rest, respite, repose on this earth, I've looked high and low, but couldn't find it, except perhaps in out-of-the-way nooks with out-of-the-ordinary books." —W.G.

DIVISION OF CHAPTERS

The Latin original of *Consolations / Soliloquy* has twenty-five chapters of uneven length. This English translation has fifty-seven chapters of comparatively even length. This has been achieved by dividing, where possible, the longish Latin chapters into several parts. Here's a schedule of the changes.

English	Latin	English	Latin	English	Latin
Prologue		20.	10.	40.	18.
1.	1.	21.	11.	41.	18.
2.	1.	22.	11.	42.	18.
3.	1.	23.	11.	43.	19.
4.	1.	24.	12.	44.	20.
5.	2.	25.	12.	45.	20.
6.	2.	26.	12.	46.	21.
7.	3.	27.	13.	47.	21.
8.	3.	28.	13.	48.	22.
9.	4.	29.	14.	49.	22.
10.	4.	30.	15.	50.	23.
11.	5.	31.	15.	51.	24.
12.	5.	32.	15.	52.	24.
13.	6.	33.	16.	53.	25.
14.	6.	34.	16.	54.	25.
15.	7.	35.	16.	55.	25.
16.	7.	36.	16.	56.	25.
17.	8.	37.	17.	57	25.
18.	9.	38.	17.	Epilogue	25.
19.	10.	39.	17.		

Selected Bibliography

Thomas à Kempis

Opera Omnia Thomae Hemerken a Kempis. Edited by M. J. Pohl. 7 vols. Freiburg: Herder, 1902–1922.

The Chronicles of the Canons Regular of Mount St. Agnes. Translated by J. P. Arthur. London: Kegan, Paul, Trench, Trübner, 1906.

The Founders of the New Devotion, Being the Lives of Gerard Groote, Florentius Radewin and Their Followers. Translated by J. P. Arthur. London: Kegan, Paul, Trench, Trübner, 1905.

A Meditation on the Incarnation of Christ: Sermons on the Life and Passion of Our Lord, and of Hearing and Speaking Good Words. Translated by Dom Vincent Scully, C.R.L. London: Kegan Paul, Trench, Trübner, 1907.

Meditations on the Life of Christ. Translated and edited by the Venerable Archdeacon Wright and the Rev. S. Kettlewell. With a Preface by the latter. New York: E. P. Dutton & Company, 1892.

Sources

Butler D. *Thomas à Kempis: A Religious Study.* London: Anderson & Ferrier, 1908.

Cruise, F. R. *Thomas à Kempis: Notes of a Visit to the Scenes in Which His Life Was Spent.* London: K. Paul, 1887.

Durant, Will. *The Reformation: A History of European Civilization from Wyclif to Calvin: 1300–1564.* New York: Simon and Schuster, 1957.

Huizinga, Johan. *The Waning of the Middle Ages: A Study of the Forms of Life, Thought, and Art in France and the Netherlands in the Dawn of the Renaissance.* New York: Doubleday Anchor Books, 1949, 1954.

Hyma, Albert. *The Brethren of the Common Life.* Grand Rapids, Mich.: Wm. B. Eerdmans, 1950.

———. *The Christian Renaissance: A History of the "Devotio Moderna."* 1st ed. New York, 1925. 2nd ed. Hamden, Conn.: Archon Books, 1965.

Kettlewell, Samuel. *Thomas à Kempis and the Brothers of Common Life.* London: K. Paul, Trench, 1882.

Le Goff, Jacques. *Medieval Civilization: 400–1500.* New York: Barnes & Noble Books, 1964, 2000.

Montmorency, J. E. G. de. *Thomas à Kempis: His Age and His Book*. London: Methuen, 1906.

Raitt, Jill, with Bernard McGinn and John Meyendorff, editors. *Christian Spirituality: High Middle Ages and Reformation*. Vol. 2 in the World Spirituality series. New York: Crossroad, 1987.

Scully, Vincent. *Life of the Venerable Thomas à Kempis, Canon Regular of St. Augustine*. With Introduction by Francis Cruise. London: R.&T. Washbourne, 1902.

Tuchman, Barbara W. *A Distant Mirror: The Calamitous 14th Century*. New York: Alfred A. Knopf, 1978.

Van Engen, J., editor. *Devotio Moderna: Basic Writings*. Preface by Heiko A. Oberman. New York: Paulist Press, 1988.

Articles, Chapters, Essays, Introductions, Prefaces

Alberts, Wybe Jappe. "Brethren of the Common Life." In *New Catholic Encyclopedia* (1967), 2:788–790.

Bangley, Bernard, trans. "Foreword" and "Afterword." In *Growing in His Image: The Imitation of Christ by Thomas À Kempis*, 9–15, 151–155. Wheaton, Ill.: Harold Shaw Publishers, 1983.

Burrows, Mark. "*Devotio Moderna:* Reforming Piety in the Later Middle Ages." In *Spiritual Traditions for the Contemporary Church*, edited by Robin Maas and Gabriel O'Donnell, O.P., chap. 4, 109–132. Nashville: Abingdon Press, 1990.

Creasy, William C., translator. "Introduction." In *The Imitation of Christ, Thomas à Kempis*, 11–27. Notre Dame, Ind.: Ave Maria Press, 1989.

Cunneen, Sally. "Preface." In *The Imitation of Christ*, translated by Joseph N. Tylenda, S.J., xv–xxvi. New York: Vintage Books, 1998.

García-Villoslada, S.J., Ricardo. "Devotio Moderna." In *New Catholic Encyclopedia* (1967) 4:831–832.

Gardiner, S.J., Harold C. "Introduction." In *The Imitation of Christ*, 5–19. New York: Doubleday Image Books, 1955.

Griffin, William. "In Praise of Paraphrase." *Books & Culture* (September–October 2002): 28–29.

Gründler, Otto. "Devotio Moderna." In *Christian Spirituality: High Middle Ages and Reformation*, edited by Jill Raitt, 176–193. New York: Crossroad, 1987.

Helms, Hal M., translator. "Introduction" and "Appendix: Rule of St. Augustine." In *The Imitation of Christ by Thomas à Kempis*, xi–xix, 250–251. Orleans, Mass.: Paraclete Press, 1982.

Klein, Edward J., editor. "Introduction." In *The Imitation of Christ: From the First Edition of an English Translation Made c. 1530 by Richard Whitford*, xi–lx. New York: Harper & Brothers, 1941.

Knox, Ronald A. "Preface." In *The Imitation of Christ by Thomas à Kempis*, translated by Ronald A. Knox, with Michael Oakley, 5–9. New York: Sheed & Ward, 1959.

Mulhern, O.P., Philip Fabian. "Thomas À Kempis." In *New Catholic Encyclopedia* (1967), 14:121–122.

Rooney, John, translator. "Translator's Preface." In *The Imitation of Christ by Thomas à Kempis*, viii–xiv. Springfield, Ill.: Templegate, 1980.

Scully, Vincent. "Thomas à Kempis." *The Catholic Encyclopedia* (1912), 14:661–663.

Steere, Douglas V. "The *Imitation of Christ*." In *Doors into Life, Through Five Devotional Classics*, chap. 1, 17–51. New York: Harper & Brothers, 1948, 1981.

Tylenda S.J., Joseph N. "Introduction." In *The Imitation of Christ in Four Books*, 13–26. Wilmington Del.: Michael Glazier, 1984.

Van Engen, John, translator. "Introduction." In *Devotio Moderna: Basic Writings*. Preface by Heiko A. Oberman, 7–35. New York: Paulist Press, 1988.

Bibles

Biblia Sacra, juxta Vulgatam Clementinam, divisionibus, summariis et concordantiis ornata. Rome: Tornaci; Paris: Desclée et Socii, 1927.

Holy Bible, The. New Revised Standard Version. New York: Oxford University Press, 1989.

Knox, Ronald A., trans. *The Holy Bible: A Translation from the Latin Vulgate in the Light of the Hebrew and Greek Originals*. New York: Sheed & Ward, 1954.

About the Translator

William Griffin has been an editor in two New York publishing houses (Harcourt and Macmillan), a literary agent in New Orleans (Southern Writers), and a magazine journalist (*Publishers Weekly*). He has done major biographical work on C. S. Lewis, G. K. Chesterton, and Billy Graham. He has anthologized the works of all three and written three novels and a number of short stories.

Recently, with thirteen years of Latin study behind him, he has taken to translating medieval and Renaissance spiritual classics into truly modern English: The *Imitation of Christ* by Thomas à Kempis; *Sermons to the People: Advent, Christmas, New Year's, Epiphany* by Augustine of Hippo; and *Short Shrifts: A Brief Life of Augustine of Hippo in His Own Words*. He was also originator of *Verbum Diurnum*, a Latin Word-for-the-Day on the Internet.

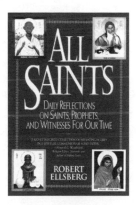

OF RELATED INTEREST

THE PRESENCE OF GOD SERIES
Bernard McGinn

In 1982, Bernard McGinn approached The Crossroad Publishing
Company with the idea for a multivolume work on the history of
Christian mysticism from the time of Jesus to the present day. The
series that has resulted is the most widely read, comprehensive, and
respected history of Christian mysticism in English, acclaimed by
scholars around the world as "classic," "brilliant," and "monumen-
tal." We proudly offer the first three volumes of McGinn's series, as
follows:

THE FOUNDATIONS OF MYSTICISM
Origins to the Fifth Century
0-8245-1404-1, $34.95 paperback

THE GROWTH OF MYSTICISM
Gregory the Great Through the Twelfth Century
0-8245-1628-1, $29.95 paperback

THE FLOWERING OF MYSTICISM
Men and Women in the New Mysticism 1200–1350
0-8245-1743-1, $34.95 paperback

**Bernard McGinn and
Patricia Ferris McGinn
EARLY CHRISTIAN MYSTICS**
The Divine Vision of the Spiritual Masters

The core message of the Church's early mystics, with reflections on
what we can learn from them for our lives today. From the world's
best-known interpreter of Christian mysticism.

0-8245-2106-4, $18.95 paperback

crossroad